BUSINESS ECONOMICS IN A RAPIDLY-CHANGING WORLD

IMPACTS OF OFFSHORING ON JOBS AND SMALL U.S. MANUFACTURERS

Business Economics in a Rapidly - Changing World

Additional books in this series can be found on Nova's website under the Series tab.

Additional E-books in this series can be found on Nova's website under the E-books tab.

Economic Issues, Problems and Perspectives

Additional books in this series can be found on Nova's website under the Series tab.

Additional E-books in this series can be found on Nova's website under the E-books tab.

BUSINESS ECONOMICS IN A RAPIDLY-CHANGING WORLD

IMPACTS OF OFFSHORING ON JOBS AND SMALL U.S. MANUFACTURERS

Jonathan S. Krekl
EDITOR

Nova Science Publishers, Inc.
New York

For permission to use material from this book please contact us:
Telephone 631-231-7269; Fax 631-231-8175
Web Site: http://www.novapublishers.com

NOTICE TO THE READER

Additional color graphics may be available in the e-book version of this book.

Library of Congress Cataloging-in-Publication Data

Impacts of offshoring on jobs and small U.S. manufacturers / editor, Jonathan S. Krekl.
p. cm.
Includes index.
ISBN 978-1-60876-064-0 (hbk.)
1. Offshore outsourcing--United States. 2. Labor market--United States. 3. Unemployment--United States. 4. Small business--United States. I. Krekl, Jonathan S.
HD2368.U6I47 2011
331.13'7973--dc23

2011033099

Published by Nova Science Publishers, Inc. † New York

CONTENTS

Preface		**iv**
Chapter 1	Offshoring (or Offshore Outsourcing) Job Loss among U.S. Workers *Lind Levine*	**1**
Chapter 2	Offshoring and U.S. Small Manufacturers Small Business Research Summary, Office of Advocacy *Small Business Research Summary, Office of Advocacy*	**25**
Index		**97**

PREFACE

Offshoring, also known as offshore outsourcing, is the term now being used to describe a practice among companies located in the United States of contracting with businesses beyond U.S. borders to perform services that would otherwise have been provided by in-house employees in white-collar occupations. The term is equally applicable to U.S. firms offshoring the jobs of blue-collar workers on textile and auto assembly lines, for example, which has been taking place for decades. The extension of offshoring from U.S. manufacturers to service providers has heightened public policy concerns about the extent of job loss and foregone employment opportunities among U.S. workers. This concern is especially pertinent to policymakers because of a national unemployment rate persistently exceeding 9% despite the end of the latest recession. This book discusses the impacts of offshoring on jobs and small U.S. manufacturers.

Chapter 1- Offshoring, also known as offshore outsourcing, is the term now being used to describe a practice among companies located in the United States of contracting with businesses beyond U.S. borders to perform services that would otherwise have been provided by in-house employees in white-collar occupations (e.g., computer systems designers). The term is equally applicable to U.S. firms offshoring the jobs of blue-collar workers on textile and auto assembly lines, for example, which has been taking place for decades. The extension of offshoring from U.S. manufacturers to service providers has heightened public policy concerns about the extent of job loss and foregone employment opportunities among U.S. workers. This concern is especially pertinent to policymakers because of a national unemployment rate persistently exceeding 9% despite the end of the latest recession in June 2009.

Chapter 2- Small manufacturers are critical to the health and dynamism of U.S. manufacturing. In 2003, manufacturers with fewer than 500 employees accounted for 99 percent of all manufacturing firms and for 43 percent of all manufacturing jobs. Small manufacturers play key roles in value-chains as suppliers to larger companies, and are often the source of many product and process innovations. (For example, small firms produce 13 to 14 times more patents per employee than larger firms.) Among the many issues affecting small manufacturers, the outsourcing of manufacturing processes overseas has been one of the most widely debated, yet little researched. This paper represents a preliminary attempt at examining the role that small firms play in manufacturing and how they have been affected by trends in outsourcing of production activities.

In: Impacts of Offshoring on Jobs …
Editor: Jonathan S. Krekl
ISBN: 978-1-60876-064-0

Chapter 1

OFFSHORING (OR OFFSHORE OUTSOURCING) AND JOB LOSS AMONG U.S. WORKERS*

Lind Levine

SUMMARY

Offshoring, also known as offshore outsourcing, is the term now being used to describe a practice among companies located in the United States of contracting with businesses beyond U.S. borders to perform services that would otherwise have been provided by in-house employees in white-collar occupations (e.g., computer systems designers). The term is equally applicable to U.S. firms offshoring the jobs of blue-collar workers on textile and auto assembly lines, for example, which has been taking place for decades. The extension of offshoring from U.S. manufacturers to service providers has heightened public policy concerns about the extent of job loss and foregone employment opportunities among U.S. workers. This concern is especially pertinent to policymakers because of a national unemployment rate persistently exceeding 9% despite the end of the latest recession in June 2009.

The outsourcing of service sector jobs within the United States was a response to the early 1980s recessions when employers narrowed their

* This is an edited, reformatted and augmented version of a Congressional Research Service publication, CRS Report for Congress RL32292, from www.crs.gov, dated on January 21, 2011.

focus to the company's core mission and contracted out peripheral activities (e.g., janitorial duties) to other U.S. businesses. The 2001 recession prompted employers to seek further efficiencies by tapping into the global supply of labor. U.S. businesses were able to outsource abroad the jobs of white-collar workers in some service-providing industries as a result of widely disseminated technological advancements that permit low cost, good quality, and high speed transmission of voice and data comm. unications. Events, such as the educational systems of comparatively low-wage nations graduating large supplies of highly educated individuals, also occurred in the intervening years which enhanced the ability of other countries (e.g., India and China) to export services to the United States.

U.S. workers reportedly have become more concerned about the security of their jobs due to increased global economic integration since the early 2000s. Offshore outsourcing, which is one manifestation of globalization, is reported to have adversely affected the employment situations of U.S. white-collar workers in information technology (IT) jobs (e.g., computer systems analysts and software engineers) and IT-enabled jobs (e.g., telemarketers and accounting clerks). Data from the U.S. Bureau of Labor Statistics' Displaced Worker Survey nevertheless suggest that the vulnerability to job loss of white-collar workers preceded the expansion of offshoring from jobs in manufacturing industries to jobs in professional and business services, administrative support services, and financial services industries. In addition, the data on displaced workers that include the latest recession suggest that macroeconomic conditions rather than offshoring have likely accounted for most of the increase in job losses in recent years.

Congress historically has striven to assist workers who lose jobs through no fault of their own, whether the job losses are caused by economy-wide downturns (i.e., cyclical unemployment) or by shifts in the industry composition of jobs performed in the United States (i.e., structural unemployment). Some observers have expressed concern that federal employment policies may not be up to the task of assisting displaced workers who must adjust to the changing mix of U.S. jobs in order to become reemployed. The wide-ranging estimates that have been developed of the number of workers in jobs that are vulnerable to being offshored provide limited guidance to Congress in its deliberations about whether existing programs to assist displaced workers are sufficient or should be expanded.

INTRODUCTION

Offshoring, also known as offshore outsourcing, initially referred to the practice of U.S. businesses contracting with firms beyond U.S. borders to provide services that would otherwise have been performed by in-house employees in white-collar occupations (e.g., computer systems designers and call center operators). However, sending abroad the jobs of blue-collar workers employed on textile and auto assembly lines, for example, has been taking place for decades. The extension of offshoring from U.S. manufacturers to service providers has heightened public policy concerns about the extent of job loss and foregone employment opportunities among U.S. workers. This concern is especially pertinent to policymakers because of a national unemployment rate persistently exceeding 9% despite the end of the latest recession in June 2009.

No regularly collected series currently provides data on the total number of U.S. workers who have lost their jobs due to offshore outsourcing, however. In 2004, the U.S. Bureau of Labor Statistics (BLS) adapted a survey of longlasting large-scale layoffs to ask firms about their movement of work to other nations.[1] Because the survey is limited to companies with at least 50 employees that have laid off workers en masse, it is more likely to capture jobs lost in manufacturing than in service-providing industries.[2]

Moreover, there is some debate about what should be considered offshoring.[3] Many observers appear to define it as the contracting out of work to non-U.S. companies located abroad and to the foreign subsidiaries of U.S. corporations. Others count as well U.S. multinational companies opening facilities overseas and importing some or all of the goods and services produced there to the United States. This conflates foreign direct investment with offshoring, however. Still others consider offshoring to include U.S. firms' purchasing services from outsourcing companies with locations in the United States (be they U.S.- or foreign-owned, such as Accenture and Wipro) that use at least some foreign workers (e.g., persons with H-1B professional specialty visas).

The short- and long-run labor market implications of offshore outsourcing are also unclear. Some observers claimed that the business practice explained much of the "jobless recovery" from the 2001 recession. Others asserted that the historical link between economic growth and job creation remained intact and, therefore, that the labor market would eventually recover from the short-run downturn in the business cycle. The labor market did in fact recover, which provided support for estimates of offshoring alone having accounted for perhaps 3% of net job loss (gross job gains minus gross job losses) early in the 2000s.[4] Some members of the public policy community are again arguing that offshoring is slowing the pace of recovery in the labor market from the 2007-2009 recession.[5]

While acknowledging that international trade and other forms of globalization (e.g., direct investment)[6] can cause painful dislocations for workers in some industries and occupations, many economists agree that it benefits the nation as a whole by enabling U.S. companies that import goods and services to sell a greater variety of higher quality products to consumers at lower prices, and by expanding markets for U.S. firms as workers in developing countries increase their demand for U.S.-made goods and services. However, some question whether this scenario applies to services offshoring. Milberg et al suggest that companies engaged in services offshoring may be its chief beneficiaries, using the profits gained from lower input costs to increase dividends to shareholders, raise stock prices through buy backs, and undertake more mergers and acquisitions to a greater degree than reinvesting and promoting growth in the U.S. economy.[7] Still others believe that domestic and offshore outsourcing have different implications for U.S. workers because firms operating in the United States are subject to federal and state minimum wage laws as well as other labor standards.[8]

Still others note that the current overseas movement of work is not defined by skill level (for which educational attainment is the commonly used proxy). In other words, the jobs of data-entry clerks and radiologists may be just as susceptible to offshoring. These individuals wonder whether offshoring will result in college graduates facing a dwindling supply of entry-level jobs that have traditionally served as stepping stones to higher skilled and higher paying positions. They also question the adequacy of the government's safety net to meet the needs of already well-educated workers who lose their jobs to offshore outsourcing.[9]

Congress historically has striven to promote U.S. job growth and assist workers who lose jobs through no fault of their own, whether job losses are caused by economy-wide downturns (i.e., cyclical unemployment) or by shifts in the industry composition of jobs performed in the United States (i.e., structural unemployment). The notion that offshoring depresses job growth in the United States appears to underlie support among some policymakers for measures meant to encourage U.S. firms to expand employment domestically rather than abroad.[10] While some members of the public policy community also support the adoption by other countries of trade and labor policies intended to level the playing field for U.S. companies and workers in the international marketplace, still others advocate for limited government intervention as the best means of promoting economic growth.[11] In addition, while most economists (trade and labor alike) support federal policies to assist those adversely affected by shifts in the nature of U.S. jobs,[12] some are also concerned that existing retraining and income support programs may not be up to the task of helping workers who are displaced by the transfer of work abroad.[13]

This report does not attempt to sort through all the issues raised above, some of which are addressed in the above-referenced CRS reports. Instead, it begins by examining the antecedents of offshore outsourcing. The report next synthesizes the literature on offshoring, focusing on implications for employment in the United States. It closes with an analysis of data since the 1980s from the BLS's Displaced Worker Survey to determine the factors that appear to be associated with increases in the risk of workers being laid off from jobs to which they are unlikely to return.

The Development of Domestic and Offshore Outsourcing

The overseas relocation of manufacturing work predates by decades the recent wave of offshoring service-providing jobs.[14] Major U.S. companies, initially responding to heightened competition from Japanese and European multinational corporations, opened facilities abroad during the 1970s and 1980s that turned out goods formerly produced by comparatively well paid, often unionized U.S. factory workers (e.g., assembly-line workers in the auto industry).

Additionally, U.S. companies reacted to the back-to-back recessions of the early 1980s by focusing on their core missions and contracting out activities that specialized domestic enterprises could perform more efficiently (e.g., janitorial services). Firms also restructured their operations by outsourcing jobs to employees of temporary help agencies, professional and business services establishments (e.g., accounting firms), and independent contractors. U.S. demand for employment (including temporary help) services continued to increase during the 1990s. It is projected to be one of the industries experiencing the most job growth in future years,[15] thus indicating that domestic outsourcing of formerly in-house functions is a permanent reorganization of how work is performed.

The 2001 recession prompted employers to achieve further efficiencies by taking advantage of technological innovations that minimize the importance of physical distance between companies. The now widespread dissemination of technologies that enable relatively low cost, good quality, and high speed transmission of voice and data communications has enabled U.S. firms to extend offshoring beyond the factory jobs of blue-collar workers to the service jobs of white-collar workers (e.g., computer programmers and call center operators). Service-providing jobs at risk of being offshored thus are both those held by information technology (IT) workers and IT-enabled workers.

Events during the intervening decade of the 1990s enhanced the ability of other countries to export services—particularly IT services—to the United States and other developed countries (e.g., the United Kingdom). One such event was addressing the so-called Y2K crisis: U.S. firms, in response to a tight supply of computer programmers in the late 1990s, turned to companies principally located in India to make the code fixes needed to avert problems with computer systems when the year 2000 arrived; the domestic firms that utilized these programmers reportedly were pleased with the quality of their work.[16]

Another event was the educational systems of low-wage foreign nations graduating an abundant supply of well educated (sometimes English-speaking) individuals.[17] In some cases, the number of persons with IT and accounting skills reportedly exceeded the immediate needs of their local economies (e.g., China, Eastern Europe, India, and the Philippines).[18] With English the language of the computer industry worldwide, IT services can be provided from many non-English-speaking, comparatively low-wage nations (e.g., Argentina, Brazil, Bulgaria, China, the Czech Republic, Hungary, Jordan, Lithuania, Mexico, Slovenia, Russia, and Ukraine).

Current and Future Prospects for Offshoring Jobs

Reasons for Increased Job Insecurity

Concern about job security has grown due in part to increased global economic integration since the early 2000s, when offshoring started spreading from the jobs of blue-collar manufacturing workers to those of white-collar service sector workers.[19] White-collar workers comprise the majority of all

U.S. workers and most white-collar workers are employed in the service sector, which accounts for the vast majority of total U.S. employment.[20] In other words, many more people today may believe their jobs are at risk of being transferred overseas.[21]

The loss of U.S. jobs to offshoring has led people to ask what field is going to be the next generator of jobs for U.S. workers, and more particularly, of "good" jobs. Because the question is not easily answered, it may exacerbate people's anxiety. The job-generating candidates that have been put forth, such as nanotechnology and biotechnology, may not provide as many new jobs as are thought to be moving abroad; further, life sciences jobs have themselves begun to be sent overseas.[22] Although U.S. workers have been encouraged to upgrade their skills so they can perform the jobs expected to be created by further U.S. technological innovation,[23] an oft-posed question in response to this advice is: in what occupations? The acquisition of IT skills had been strongly advocated for several years; however, these are among the jobs that appear newly at risk of being offshored. If both high-skilled and low-skilled work is vulnerable to offshoring, then one's field of study may be as (or perhaps more) important than the level of education attained.[24]

How Many Jobs Are We Talking About?

People have questioned whether we are seeing the initial leakage of service-providing jobs from the United States, with many more to follow in an expanding range of white-collar occupations. The query has elicited very different replies and produced a wide range of empirical estimates and anecdotal evidence.

Offshoring of white-collar jobs initially involved "simple service work, like processing credit-card receipts, and mind-numbing digital toil, like writing software code."[25] It reportedly has expanded to such functions as processing home loans of U.S. mortgage applicants, interpreting CT scans of U.S. hospital patients, and preparing corporate financial analyses for U.S. investors. According to one survey conducted for several years that covers a wide range of firms by size and industry, employers are increasingly willing to send overseas "highly skilled innovation activities," such as "product design, R&D, engineering services, and software development."[26]

Forrester Research, Inc. was the source of perhaps the first and most commonly cited statistics on offshoring. According to its forecast that appears to have been based on discussions with experts, a total of 3.4 million service sector jobs might move abroad by 2015.[27] As shown in Table 1, Forrester projected in 2004 that a total of 1.2 million services jobs might be relocated offshore between 2003 and 2008. Of this five-year total, computer occupations might represent one of every five offshored positions. Beyond 2008, Forrester did not provide data in one-year intervals. It did forecast that by 2010 a total of 1.7 million jobs might have gone offshore, for a two-year increase of one-half million. Adding to that Forrester's projected transfer over the next five years of another 1.7 million jobs, a grand total of 3.4 million jobs might move offshore by 2015. However, Bhagwati et al point out that Forrester's forecasted loss of some 300,000 jobs per year on average represents a very small share of the jobs typically created and destroyed each year in the United States.[28]

Table 1. Cumulative Number of U.S. Service Sector Jobs Forecast to Shift Offshore, by Occupational Group (numbers in thousands)

Occupational Group	2003	2004	2005	2006	2007	2008
Administrative support	146	256	410	475	541	616
Computer	102	143	181	203	228	247
Business and financial operations	30	55	91	105	120	136
Management	3.5	15	34	42	48	64
Sales	11	22	38	47	55	67
Architecture	14	27	46	54	61	70
Legal	6	12	20	23	26	29
Life sciences	0.3	2	4	5.5	6.5	9
Art, design and related	2.5	4.5	8	9	10	11
Total	315	540	830	960	1,100	1,200

Source: Adapted by CRS from John C. McCarthy, *Near-Term Growth of Offshoring Accelerating*, Forrester Research, Inc., May 14, 2004.

Bardhan and Kroll estimated that more than 14 million jobs, representing about 11% of U.S. employment in 2001, have attributes that could allow them to be sent overseas (e.g., no in-person customer servicing required; an IT-enabled work process that can be accomplished via telecommuting; jobs that can be routinized; a fairly wide gap between a job's pay in the United States compared to in a destination country; and a destination country having few language, institutional, and cultural barriers).[29] While these jobs are at risk of being offshored, the number represents an outer limit according to the authors. The occupational groups identified as being susceptible to offshoring include office support (e.g., data entry and payroll clerks), auditors and tax preparers, computer programmers and software engineers, medical transcriptionists and paralegals, and technical writers. They are concentrated in such industries as information, finance and insurance, and professional and business services.

A study released by the Brookings Institution built upon the work of Bardhan and Kroll, Forrester Research, and others to develop projections of the share of jobs in 246 metropolitan areas that might be lost due to services offshoring over the 2004-2015 period. The researchers concluded that offshoring may not greatly affect employment in most metropolitan areas, with just 2.2% of the jobs in these 246 areas likely to be offshored between 2004 and 2015.[30] The analysis suggests that five metro areas might lose somewhat more jobs (between 3.1% and 4.3%) by 2015: Boulder, CO; Lowell, MA; San Francisco, CA; San Jose, CA; and Stamford, CT. Another 23 areas might have between 2.6% and 3.0% of their jobs offshored. Those metropolitan areas estimated to be most vulnerable to services offshoring tend to be very populous, having 1 million or more inhabitants (e.g., Dallas, TX; Minneapolis, MN; and Washington, DC). They also tend to be located in the Northeast (e.g., Bergen-Passaic, NJ; Boston, MA; and Hartford, CT) and West (e.g., Denver, CO and San Jose, CA). In addition, they generally have high concentrations of IT jobs (e.g., Boulder, CO; Huntsville, AL; and Lowell, MA) or IT-enabled back-office jobs such as data-entry keyers and telemarketers (e.g., Des Moines, IA; Omaha, NE; and Wilmington, DE).

Jensen and Kletzer developed a different geographically based approach to estimate the share of tradable (offshorable) and nontradable (nonoffshorable) jobs in manufacturing and nonmanufacturing (e.g., agriculture, mining, construction, services) industries. About 9.4% of total U.S. employment in 2000 was found to be in offshorable industries, according to one of their estimates.[31] More specifically, 13.7% of employment in professional services industries might be vulnerable to offshoring compared to 12.4% of employment in manufacturing industries.

Jensen and Kletzer examined the data by occupation as well. They estimated that at least 60% of workers in the following occupations may be susceptible to offshoring: computer and mathematical; legal; life, physical, and social sciences; business and financial operations; and architecture and engineering. Jensen and Kletzer suggested that because white-collar occupations often involve potentially offshorable activities and they may be shed by nontradable industries, the industry results in the preceding paragraph might understate the percentage of workers at risk of having their jobs offshored.[32]

BLS undertook an examination of the vulnerability to offshoring of service-providing occupations in particular. Out of 515 occupations, BLS estimated that 160 may be susceptible to transfer offshore. More than one-half of these offshorable occupations are in various professional and technical categories, with virtually all computer and mathematical science occupations being to some degree vulnerable to offshoring. In 2007, there were some 30 million jobs in these 160 offshorable service-providing occupations; they accounted for over one-fifth of total employment in that year. Despite their vulnerability to being offshored, employment in these occupations grew slightly faster than overall service-providing employment in the 2001-2007 period. In addition, wage growth was comparatively greater in these offshorable occupations between 2001 and 2007. However, the 33 service-providing occupations found to be most susceptible to offshoring experienced below average employment and wage growth during the period. The skills and education of this most vulnerable group range widely:

> Fifteen are office and administrative support occupations [e.g., bookkeeping, accounting, and auditing clerks], with relatively low education or training requirements. Another 11 are professional and related occupations [e.g., computer operators, programmers, and support specialists], which generally possess higher educational requirements.[33]

Blinder also took an occupational approach and created an index of offshorability for hundreds of blue-collar, white-collar, and service occupations based on the degree to which the jobs required persons to be located physically close to a U.S. work location. He estimated that a majority of occupations (533) and employed persons (92.6 million in 2004) are *non*offshorable—that is, they are completely immune to offshoring (see category IV in Table 2). Conversely, Blinder estimated that a minority of U.S. occupations (about 200) and workers (almost 30 million) fall in the highly offshorable and offshorable categories. He considered the two categories, which included 22.2% of U.S. workers in 2004, too conservative an estimate of potentially offshorable jobs in light of technological and other advances expected to arise in the coming years. Blinder added to the conservative estimate those occupations in category III he ranked as most susceptible to being offshored to create a moderate estimate totaling 25.6% of all U.S.

workers. His aggressive estimate includes all of category III and totals almost 40 million workers or 29.0% of all U.S. jobs. Blinder goes on to say that "Contrary to conventional wisdom, the more offshorable occupations are not low-end jobs, whether measured by wages or by education. The correlation between skill and offshorability is almost zero."[34] This conclusion is supported by the above-described research of BLS economists.

Blinder and Krueger used three alternative survey methods to try to determine how many of the jobs that workers held in 2008 were vulnerable to being moved overseas. All three methods found that about one in four U.S. jobs may be potentially offshorable.[35] Their analysis suggests that offshorability is especially prevalent in factory and administrative support jobs, and on an industry basis, in manufacturing, finance, information, and professional services.

Table 2. Occupational Categories by Degree of Offshorability

		Occupations		
Category	Degree of Offshorability	Examples	Number of Occupations	2004 Employment (in millions)
I	Highly offshorable	computer programmers and systems analysts; telemarketers; bookkeeping, accounting, and auditing clerks	59	8.2
II	Offshorable	computer software engineers; accountants; machine operators, team assemblers and production worker helpers; bill and account collectors	151	20.7
III	Hard to offshore	general and operations managers; stock clerks and order fillers; shipping, receiving, and traffic clerks	74	8.8
IV	Non-offshorable	business operations specialists; health and safety engineers; music directors; photographers; postal service mail sorters	533	92.6
Total			817	130.0

Source: Alan S. Blinder, "How Many US Jobs Might be Offshorable?," *World Economics*, vol. 10, no. 2 (April-June 2009).

There are others who believe fears about services offshoring have been overblown. One explanation for why perhaps only one-tenth of the potential market for offshoring global IT and business processes work was realized through 2006 is that "executives have a lot to learn about using offshore talent to boost productivity.... The management challenge will grow more urgent as rising global salaries dissipate the easy cost gains from offshore outsourcing."[36] Some, therefore, are cautious about the future pace of moving abroad potentially vulnerable U.S. jobs. For example, Deloitte Consulting concluded that

> outsourcing will lose "holy grail" status. In the future, companies will not outsource because it is the latest management fad.... Organizations will carefully define core, strategic, and "thought-leadership" functions and will keep those inhouse to retain knowledge, confidentiality, and control over key functions. Some organizations will decide to outsource only short-term.... Many organizations will also engage in large scale re-insourcing thereby further eroding the outsourcing market.[37]

Dell, for example, returned some help services to the United States due to customer dissatisfaction.[38] Other U.S. firms reportedly had to employ IT service providers located in the United States to fix software produced abroad.[39]

Some employers may have overestimated the cost savings from outsourcing because a service's purchase price is affected by more than inter-country wage differentials, such as travel and managerial oversight costs. META Group noted that some firms estimate labor cost savings by making a "person-to-person comparison (e.g., a full-time equivalent in India will cost 40% less)" and ignoring "hidden costs and differences in operating models" that may reduce savings.[40]

At least two factors that could have put the brakes on offshoring have failed to do so, however. Offshore providers of IT services, for example, were able to allay U.S. firms' fears about security shortly after the terrorist attacks of September 11, 2001.[41] Despite 9/11, U.S. airline carriers have continued their "increased outsourcing of maintenance jobs overseas—to places like Singapore, Brazil, the Dominican Republic—not only for international aircraft but even for planes on purely domestic routes."[42] In addition, concern periodically has arisen among U.S. outsourcers over unrest in some regions (e.g., disputes between India and Pakistan as well as in the Middle East). Global providers of software services have responded by placing more of their clients' work in a variety of countries, including the "near-shore" markets of Canada and Mexico.[43] Some individual U.S. employers also reportedly believe that moving work to nearby Canada, which has fewer cultural differences with the United States than India or the Philippines for example, likely reduces their customers' potential antipathy to offshoring.[44]

In summary, empirical analyses have produced a wide range of estimates of how many U.S. workers might be displaced because their jobs have characteristics that make them susceptible to offshoring. Because these estimates are so different in magnitude, they provide little guidance to Congress about whether existing worker adjustment and retraining programs are sufficient or should be expanded in some way (e.g., increase appropriations for federal retraining programs and extend the social safety net to all displaced workers, not just those who lose their jobs to foreign competition),[45] and if the latter, by when the expansion should take place. The studies do agree, however, that potential job losses are likely to be concentrated in particular occupations and industries because offshoring appears to change the composition of goods produced and services provided in the United States. Such restructuring of the labor market further suggests that some of the workers displaced by offshoring will have to change fields to obtain new jobs, which could prolong their period of unemployment.[46]

Trends in Worker Displacement

As the United States transitioned during the 20th century from an agrarian to an industrial economy and then to a service economy, the evolving structure of the labor market has fueled workers' concern about job loss. The data presented below from the Displaced Worker Survey (DWS), which was begun by the BLS in the early 1980s, support the impression that the composition of jobs in the U.S. labor market has changed. Generally speaking, the DWS data show that white-collar workers in some service-providing industries have become more vulnerable within the past few decades to permanently losing their jobs. But, the timing of white-collar workers' increased risk of displacement preceded the extension of offshoring from manufacturing to service-providing industries.[47] (See the box below for a description of the displaced worker population.)

In addition, prevailing macroeconomic conditions rather than offshoring have likely accounted for most of the recent runup in unemployment given the widespread increase in displacement. Although U.S. companies have conducted a dwindling number of mass layoffs since the recession's end in June 2009,[48] the national unemployment rate has been above 9% for more than a year into the slow-paced recovery from the 2007-2009 recession.[49]

1981-2000

The risk of job loss among manufacturing industry workers improved from 1981-1982 to 1991-1992, two comparable periods in that they included recessions. As the economy recovered from the severe 1981-1982 recession, the chance of losing a manufacturing job subsequently decreased. During the milder 1990-1991 recession, the displacement rate[50] among manufacturing workers rose to 7.1% but did not reach its 1981-1982 level of 8.2%. (See top panel of Table 3.)

In contrast, the job security of most other workers worsened or stayed about the same over the 10- year period. The incidence of permanent layoffs in finance, insurance, and real estate quadrupled to 5.5%. The displacement rate also climbed (but less steeply) in the construction, wholesale and retail trade, and services industries. But, none of the service sector industries was close to the risk of job loss in 1991-1992 of construction (8.4%) or manufacturing (7.1%).

> *Displaced workers* are persons at least 20 years old who had worked for their employers at least three years before losing their jobs because of plant or company closings and moves, insufficient work for them to do, or abolishment of their positions and shifts. The definition is intended to identify workers who had some attachment to their employers, were terminated through no fault of their own, and who did not expect to be recalled to their former jobs.
>
> Source: U.S. Bureau of Labor Statistics, *Worker Displacement: 2007-2009*, August 26, 2010.

The shift in the pattern of displacement toward service-providing industries translated into a change in displacement's occupational distribution in light of the predominance of blue-collar workers at manufacturers and white-collar workers at service providers. The risk of permanent job loss was lower among blue-collar workers in the 1991-1992 period (5.3%) compared to the 1981-1982 period. At the same time, it rose to 3.7% from 2.6% among white-collar workers. (See bottom panel of Table 3.)

Table 3. Displacement Rates by Industry and Occupation of Lost Job, 1981-1982 and 1991-1992

Characteristic		1981-1982	1991-1992
All long-tenured workers age 20 and older		3.9	3.9
	Industry		
Mining		13.6	7.4
Construction		7.6	8.4
Manufacturing		8.2	7.1
Transportation and public utilities		4.1	4.4
Wholesale and retail trade		3.7	4.7
Finance, insurance, and real estate		1.4	5.5
Services		2.3	2.9
Government		1.2	1.1
Agriculture		5.4	3.8
	Occupation		
White-collar workers		2.6	3.7
Managerial and professional specialty		2.1	3.6
—Executive, administrative, and managerial		2.5	4.8
—Professional specialty		1.7	2.4
Technical, sales, and administrative support		3.0	3.7
—Technicians and related support		3.3	3.7
—Sales occupations		3.7	3.6
—Administrative support, including clerical		2.5	3.8
Blue-collar workers		7.3	5.3
Service workers		2.0	2.1
Farming, forestry, and fishing		0.9	1.4

Source: Ryan T. Helwig, "Worker Displacement in 1999-2000," *Monthly Labor Review*, June 2004.

White-collar workers whose risk of displacement increased to the greatest extent were employed in managerial occupations and in administrative support (including clerical) occupations. The chance of job loss among executives, administrators, and managers almost doubled to 4.8%. The increased displacement of those who themselves manage companies is reported to have had a widespread psychological impact at the time because "When people on higher rungs of the corporate ladder lose their jobs, it throws fear into the hearts of thousands of workers" and represents "a corporate vote of no confidence in any worker's job security."[51] Among those in administrative support jobs, the displacement rate rose by half from 2.5% to 3.8%. The likelihood of permanent layoffs increased somewhat, to 2.4%, among professionals as well. These data lend support to the widespread belief of white-collar workers that their jobs have become less secure, but the change pre-dated any noticeable offshoring of service sector jobs.

Displacement rates fell virtually across the board during the economic expansion of the 1990s. When examined against a fairly comparable period 10 years earlier, the probability of job loss was lower at the end of the decade than at its beginning. (See Table 4.)

For the first time since the DWS data were collected, the risk of job loss among employees of the services industry group (e.g., telecommunications firms and providers of computer services to other businesses) rose to the point that it equaled the average displacement rate in 1999-2000. Bardhan and Kroll suggest that any offshoring of services that occurred at that time "can be seen as spinoffs from the US because of tight labor markets, rather than job transfers out of the US in search of lower labor costs."[52] The services offshoring that continued to occur during the subsequent 2001 recession and sluggish recovery when unemployment in the United States was more pervasive than during much of the 1990s may have "involve[d] the transfer of US jobs and occupations to other countries," however.

2001-2008

The initial years of the 2000s saw an increase in the incidence of worker displacement from the prior decade shown in Table 4, which was characterized by a booming economy. In 2001-2002, which includes the 2001 recession, the displacement rate was 4.3% (see Table 5). The displacement rate clearly exhibits a strong countercyclical pattern.

Table 4. Displacement Rates by Industry and Occupation of Lost Job, 1989-1990 and 1999-2000

Characteristic		1989-1990	1999-2000
All long-tenured workers age 20 and older		3.1	2.5
	Industry		
Mining		10.0	7.5
Construction		5.9	3.3
Manufacturing		5.0	4.7
Transportation and public utilities		3.6	2.7
Wholesale and retail trade		3.9	3.1
Finance, insurance, and real estate		3.5	3.7
Services		2.1	2.5
Government		0.4	0.5
Agriculture		3.2	1.7
	Occupation		
White-collar workers		2.7	2.4
Managerial and professional specialty		2.3	2.1
—Executive, administrative, and managerial		3.4	2.7
—Professional specialty		1.3	1.6
Technical, sales, and administrative support		3.1	2.7
—Technicians and related support		3.2	2.7
—Sales occupations		2.9	2.9
—Administration support, including clerical		3.2	2.6
Blue-collar workers		4.5	3.3
Service workers		1.6	1.4
Farming, forestry, and fishing		1.5	0.5

Source: Ryan T. Helwig, "Worker Displacement in 1999-2000," *Monthly Labor Review*, June 2004.

The risk of permanent job loss lessened through mid-decade as the labor market belatedly responded to the economic recovery from the 2001 recession. As shown in Table 5, the risk of job loss had climbed to 4.1% by 2007-2008, which includes the first year of the 2007-2009 recession. This figure about equals the displacement rate recorded during the prior recession of the decade.

Table 5. Displacement Rates by Industry and Occupation of Lost Job, 2001-2002 to 2007-2008

Characteristic	2001-2002	2003-2004	2005-2006	2007-2008
All long-tenured workers aged 20 and older	4.3	3.1	2.7	4.1
Industry				
Mining	2.3	5.5	1.6	3.2
Construction	4.1	4.6	2.5	9.1
Manufacturing	8.7	6.4	5.1	6.6
Transportation and public utilities	3.9	3.8	2.8	4.0
Wholesale and retail trade	4.8	3.2	2.7	4.7
Financial activities	3.4	4.0	3.7	6.4
Information	9.6	5.0	5.4	4.7
Professional and business services	7.1	4.1	3.0	5.2
Education and health services	2.0	1.4	1.4	2.3
Leisure and hospitality	2.6	2.4	3.4	3.3
Other services	2.8	1.9	3.6	3.0
Government	0.6	0.7	0.5	0.8
Agriculture	4.1	1.2	1.8	2.5
Occupation				
Management, professional, and related occupations	3.9	2.9	2.2	3.3
—Management, business, and financial operations occupations	5.2	4.0	2.8	4.9
—Professional and related occupations	3.1	2.2	1.9	2.3
Sales and office occupations	4.4	3.2	2.9	4.5
—Sales and related occupations	5.2	3.4	3.2	4.9
—Office and administrative support	3.9	3.0	2.7	4.3
Natural resources, construction, and maintenance occupations	5.0	3.8	2.5	6.3
—Farming, fishing, and forestry	4.2	4.0	3.3	2.4
—Construction and extraction occupations	4.4	4.0	1.9	8.1
—Installation, maintenance, and repair	5.8	4.1	3.2	4.4
Production, transportation, and material moving occupations	6.9	4.6	4.5	5.6
—Production occupations	8.7	5.3	5.9	6.6
—Transportation and material moving	4.4	3.5	2.8	4.4
Service occupations	2.2	1.6	1.6	2.7

Source: Unpublished data from the U.S. Bureau of Labor Statistics, Displaced Worker Survey.

As shown in Table 5, the information industry[53] recorded the highest rate of permanent job loss, at 9.6%, in the 2001-2002 period.[54] Another service-providing industry with a well above-average displacement rate was professional and business services, at 7.1%; some IT-intensive industries (e.g., computer systems design and related services as well as architectural and engineering services) lie within this industry group. The elevated rates of the two industries coincided with the bursting of the IT-telecom bubble. The incidence of displacement in the cyclically sensitive manufacturing rose as well to 8.7%, putting it between the two services industries. Jensen and Kletzer estimated a somewhat higher job loss rate among workers in offshorable services compared to manufacturing industries during the early years of the decade, but they note that the difference may have been caused by the dot.com bust.[55]

As the economy recovered from the 2001 recession, the risk of job loss abated across nearly all industries through mid-decade. Kletzer and Jensen, in an update to their earlier study, estimated that non-offshorable manufacturing industries had a higher displacement rate than offshorable manufacturing industries from 2003 to mid-decade. The same pattern was estimated for non-offshorable compared to offshorable services industries (i.e., information, financial, and professional and business services). Within the services industries, the displacement rate was higher in offshorable professional and business services industries compared to nonoffshorable professional and business services industries. The authors note that professional and business services nonetheless had a much lower rate of displacement compared to offshorable manufacturing industries.[56]

During the first year of the 2007-2009 recession, the displacement rate climbed in almost every industry. Displacement among workers in the construction industry quadrupled from its level in 2005-2006. At 9.1%, employees of the construction industry had the highest likelihood of being laid off. The financial activities industry, which traditionally has not been especially sensitive to fluctuations in the business cycle, reported almost a doubling of its displacement rate to 6.4% between 2005-2006 and 2007-2008. The pattern in both these industries likely reflects a unique feature of the 2007-2009 recession, namely, it is the only recession of the postwar period precipitated by interwoven crises in the financial and housing markets. Although the risk of job loss in traditionally cyclically sensitive manufacturing did not increase as greatly, the industry recorded the second highest at 6.6%.

The likelihood of losing a job fell across most occupations between the two recessions of the 2000s. During the 2001 recession, however, factory workers (i.e., those in production jobs) had the highest incidence of permanent job loss at 8.7%. The displacement rate of this cyclically sensitive occupation was the second highest during the first year of the 2007-2009 recession at 6.6%.

While the risk of job loss was about average among workers in co-nstruction occupations (e.g., carpenters, masons, roofers, and electricians) in the first recession of the decade, it was the highest of any occupation in 2007-2008 at 8.1%. Workers in construction jobs experienced the most substantial increase in risk of job loss between 2005-2006 and 2007-2008, more than quadrupling from 1.9%. This pattern largely reflects the bursting of the housing bubble that characterized the first half of the 2000s.[57] Given the attributes of construction jobs, offshoring could not have been a contributing factor to the occupation's increased likelihood of displacement.

End Notes

[1] U.S. Bureau of Labor Statistics, quarterly news releases on extended mass layoffs are available at http://stats.bls.gov/mls/. For additional information see CRS Report RL30799, *Unemployment Through Layoffs and Offshore Outsourcing*, by Linda Levine

[2] Service industries include firms that provide professional and business services (e.g., legal, accounting, engineering, and computer system design), office administrative services (e.g., billing and recordkeeping), and financial services (e.g., banks, credit card issuers, and mortgage lenders).

[3] For a review of the various meanings in the literature on offshoring see National Academy of Public Administration, *Off-Shoring: An Elusive Phenomenon*, Washington, DC, January 2006.

[4] The 3% figure was developed by William Dickens, Senior Fellow, Economic Studies, The Brookings Institution, and presented during a March 3, 2004 Brookings forum on offshoring.

[5] For example, as reported in *EPI News*, January 2011,"In a year when fewer than one million domestic jobs were created, International Economist Robert Scott [of the Economic Policy Institute] calculates that the growth in the U.S. trade deficit in 2010 created 1.4 million jobs overseas in 2010 and that many of those jobs were outsourced by American companies."

[6] For more information on foreign companies investing in the United States, see CRS Report RS21857, *Foreign Direct Investment in the United States: An Economic Analysis*, by James K. Jackson.

[7] William Milberg, Melissa Mahoney, Markus Schneider, and Rudi von Arnim, "Dynamic Gains From U.S. Services Offshoring: A Critical View," in *Global Capitalism Unbound: Winners and Losers from Offshore Outsourcing*, ed. Eva Paus (New York: Palgrave Macmillan), pp. 77-93.

[8] John Sullivan, "Forum Reveals Divisions Over Effects of Exporting U.S. Jobs to Other Countries," *Daily Labor Report*, December 12, 2003.

[9] Alan S. Blinder, "Offshoring: The Next Industrial Revolution?," *Foreign Affairs*, vol. 85, issue 2, March/April 2006, pp. 113-128 (hereinafter cited as Blinder, *Offshoring: The Next Industrial Revolution?*); and Christopher Koch, "Backlash," *CIO Magazine*, September 1, 2003.

[10] See for example CRS Report RL31444, *Firms That Incorporate Abroad for Tax Purposes: Corporate "Inversions" and "Expatriation,"* by Donald J. Marples and CRS Report 97-765, *The Buy American Act: Requiring Government Procurements to Come from Domestic Sources*, by John R. Luckey.

[11] See for example CRS Report RL34091, *Globalization, Worker Insecurity, and Policy Approaches*, by Raymond J. Ahearn.

[12] Jagdish Bhagwati and Alan S. Blinder, ed., *Offshoring of American Jobs: What Response From U.S. Economic Policy?* (Cambridge, MA: MIT Press, 2009).

[13] For information on existing worker retraining and income support programs see CRS Report RS22718, *Trade Adjustment Assistance for Workers (TAA) and Reemployment Trade Adjustment Assistance (RTAA)*, by John J. Topoleski, CRS Report RL33687, *The Workforce Investment Act (WIA): Program-by-Program Overview and Funding of Title I Training Programs*, by David H. Bradley, and CRS Report RS22538, *Unemployment Compensation: The Cornerstone of Income Support for Unemployed Workers*, by Julie M. Whittaker.

[14] Jagdish Bhagwati, Arvind Panagariya, and R.N. Srinivasan, "The Muddles Over Outsourcing," *Journal of Economic Perspectives*, vol. 18, no. 4 (Fall 2004), pp. 93-114. (Hereinafter cited as Bhagwati, Panagariya, and Srinivasan, *The Muddles Over Outsourcing*.)

[15] Rose A. Woods, "Industry Output and Employment Projections to 2018," *Monthly Labor Review*, November 2009.

[16] Jeffrey Marshall, "Outsourcing Overseas: Savings Road Leads to India," *Financial Executive*, September 2002.

[17] Richard B. Freeman, "The Challenge of the Growing Globalization of Labor Markets to Economic and Social Policy," in *Global Capitalism Unbound: Winners and Losers from Offshore Outsourcing*, ed. Eva Paus (New York: Palgrave Macmillan), pp. 23-39.

[18] Pete Engardio, Aaron Bernstein, and Manjeef Kripalani, "The New Global Job Shift," *Business Week*, February 3, 2003 (hereinafter cited as Engardio, et al., *The New Global Job Shift*.); Larry Greenemeier, "Offshore Outsourcing Grows to Global Proportions—U.S. Companies Extend Their Search Beyond India for IT Help Overseas," *InformationWeek*, February 11, 2002; and Drew Robb, "Offshore Outsourcing Nears Critical Mass—The IT Talent Shortage in the United States is Driving More Companies to Use Overseas Developers," *InformationWeek*, June 12, 2000.

[19] See for example Richard G. Anderson and Charles S. Gascon, *Offshoring, Economic Insecurity, and the Demand for Social Insurance*, Federal Reserve Bank of St. Louis, Working Paper 2008-003A, St. Louis, MO, January 2008; and William Milberg and Deborah Winkler, *Globalization, Offshoring, and Economic Insecurity in Industrialized Countries*, United Nations, Department of Economic and Social Affairs Working Paper 87, New York, NY, November 2009.

[20] According to data from the Current Population Survey, there were 86,006,000 persons employed in white-collar occupations in 2009. (White-collar occupations are management, professional, sales and office occupations.) These white-collar workers accounted for 61% of the 139,877,000 persons employed in that year.

[21] The possibility that offshoring may create jobs for U.S. workers (e.g., those who develop the contracts for outsourced activities and those who oversee their performance) does not appear to have allayed workers' concern about job security. If the overseas firms and workers who perform these contracted activities subsequently purchase goods and services from U.S. firms and make investments in the United States, their actions also may create jobs in the United States. While potentially leading to job losses in certain industries and occupations, offshoring on balance may not much affect the overall level of U.S. employment. For example, Amiti and Wei ("Does Service Offshoring Lead to Job Losses? Evidence from the United States," in Marshall Reinsdorf and Matthew J. Slaughter (eds) *International Trade in Services and Intangibles in the Era of Globalization*, (Cambridge, MA: National Bureau of Economic Research, 2009)), estimated that offshoring of services

by U.S. firms between 1992 and 2000 had little (about 0.4%) or no effect on employment levels at U.S. manufacturers.

[22] Andrew Pollack, "Medical Companies Joining Offshore Trend," *New York Times*, February 24, 2005.

[23] Clare Ansberry, "Why U.S. Manufacturing Won't Die," *Wall Street Journal*, July 3, 2003; and Steve Lohr, "Many New Causes for Old Problem of Jobs Lost Abroad," *New York Times*, February 15, 2004.

[24] Alan S. Blinder, "Offshoring: Big Deal, or Business As Usual?," in *Offshoring of American Jobs: What Response From U.S. Economic Policy?* ed. Jagdish Bhagwati and Alan S. Blinder (Cambridge, MA: MIT Press, 2009), pp. 19-59.

[25] Engardio et al., *The New Global Job Shift*, p. 50.

[26] Duke University Offshoring Research Network and The Conference Board, *2007-2008 ORN Survey Report*, Research Report 1445-09-RR, 2009, pp. 10-11.

[27] John C. McCarthy, *Near-Term Growth of Offshoring Accelerating*, Forrester Research, Inc., May 14, 2004.

[28] Bhagwati, Panagariya, and Srinivasan, *The Muddles Over Outsourcing*.

[29] Ashok Deo Bardhan and Cynthia A. Kroll, "The New Wave of Outsourcing," *Fisher Center Research Report*, University of California-Berkeley, fall 2003 (hereinafter cited as Bardhan and Kroll, *The New Wave of Outsourcing*.); and Cynthia A. Kroll, "State and Metropolitan Area Impacts of the Offshore Outsourcing of Business Services, and IT," *Fisher Center Research Report*, University of California-Berkeley, 2005. See also, C. Alan Garner," Offshoring in the Service Sector: Economic Impact and Policy Issues," Federal Reserve Bank of Kansas City's *Economic Review*, third quarter 2004.

[30] Robert Atkinson and Howard Wial, *The Implications of Service Offshoring for Metropolitan Economies*, The Brookings Institution Metropolitan Policy Program, February 2007.

[31] J. Bradford Jensen and Lori G. Kletzer, "Tradable Services: Understanding the Scope and Impact of Services Offshoring," in *Offshoring White-Collar Work—Issues and Implications*, ed. Lael Brainard and Susan M. Collins (Washington, DC: The Brookings Institution, 2005), pp. 75-116. (Hereinafter cited as Jensen and Kletzer, *Tradable Services: Understanding the Scope and Impact of Services Offshoring*.)

[32] Jensen and Kletzer, *Tradable Services: Understanding the Scope and Impact of Services Offshoring*.

[33] Roger J. Moncarz, Michael G. Wolf, and Benjamin Wright, "Service-providing Occupations, Offshoring, and the Labor Market," *Monthly Labor Review*, December 2008, pp. 76-77.

[34] Alan S. Blinder, "How Many US Jobs Might be Offshorable?," *World Economics*, vol. 10, no. 2 (April-June 2009), p. 69.

[35] Alan S. Blinder and Alan B. Krueger, *Alternative Measures of Offshorability: A Survey Approach*, National Bureau of Economic Research, Working Paper 15287, Cambridge, MA, August 2009.

[36] Peter Engardio, "The Future of Outsourcing," *Business Week*, January 30, 2006, p. 58.

[37] Deloitte Consulting, *Calling A Change in the Outsourcing Market: The Realities for the World's Largest Organizations*, April 2005, p. 25.

[38] Khozem Merchant, "Tough Call for the US Cost-Cutters," *Financial Times*, December 22, 2003.

[39] Olga Kharif, "The Hidden Costs of IT Outsourcing," *BusinessWeek online*, October 27, 2003; and Ryan B. Patrick, "Signs of Offshore Backlash Growing," *Computerworld*, January 8, 2004.

[40] "Offshore Outsourcing Cost-Savings Perceptions Differ from Realities," *Business Wire*, January 13, 2004.

[41] Julie Gallagher, "Redefining the Business Case for Offshore Outsourcing," *Insurance & Technology*, April 2002.

[42] Al Kamen, "In the Loop," *Washington Post*, February 27, 2004, p. A21.

[43] "Gartner Dataquest Says IT Outsourcing Industry to Advance with Increased Demand in Offshore Outsourcing," *Business Wire*, January 30, 2003.

[44] Ian Austen, "Canada, the Closer Country for Outsourcing Work," *New York Times*, November 30, 2004.

[45] Alan S. Blinder, "Offshoring: Big Deal, or Business As Usual?," in *Offshoring of American Jobs: What Response From U.S. Economic Policy?* ed. Jagdish Bhagwati and Alan S. Blinder (Cambridge, MA: MIT Press, 2009), pp. 19-59.

[46] Organisation for Economic Co-operation and Development, *Globalisation, Jobs and Wages*, Policy Brief, June 2007.

[47] Little attention typically is paid to the displacement of workers in such service occupations as cooks and servers, cleaners and maintenance workers, hairdressers and child care workers, and police and firefighters. Workers in service occupations are generally less likely than blue-collar and white-collar workers to be affected by offshoring because many of their jobs require face-to-face interaction with customers.

[48] U.S. Bureau of Labor Statistics, *Extended Mass Layoffs—Third Quarter 2010*, November 12, 2010.

[49] For information on the comparative pace of recovery in the labor market see CRS Report R41434, *Job Growth During the Recovery*, by Linda Levine.

[50] The displacement rate is the number of displaced workers in a particular group divided by the tenure-adjusted, two-year average estimate of employment for that same group.

[51] Perri Capell, "Endangered Middle Managers," *American Demographics*, January 1992, p. 37.

[52] Bardhan and Kroll, *The New Wave of Outsourcing*, p. 3.

[53] The information industry includes wired telecommunications carriers, radio and television broadcasting and cable, motion pictures and video, newspapers, and publishing.

[54] Because new industry and occupation classification systems were introduced, the DWS data since 2000 is not directly comparable with industry and occupation data for earlier years.

[55] Jensen and Kletzer, *Tradable Services: Understanding the Scope and Impact of Services Offshoring*.

[56] J. Bradford Jensen and Lori G. Kletzer, *"Fear" and Offshoring: The Scope and Potential Impact of Imports and Exports of Services*, Peterson Institute for International Economics, Policy Brief 08-1, Washington, DC, January 2008.

[57] For an estimate of the number of residential construction and related jobs supported by bubble-related demand in 2005, and the number of jobs that might have existed in 2008 had the bubble not occurred, see Kathryn J. Byun, "The U.S. Housing Bubble and Bust: Impacts on Employment," *Monthly Labor Review*, December 2010, pp. 3-17.

In: Impacts of Offshoring on Jobs …
Editor: Jonathan S. Krekl
ISBN: 978-1-60876-064-0

Chapter 2

OFFSHORING AND U.S. SMALL MANUFACTURERS*

Small Business Research Summary, Office of Advocacy

An Office of Advocacy Working Paper
by
StratEdge
Alexandria, VA 22302
For
Small Business Research Summary, Office of Advocacy
Under contract number SBAHQ-05-M-0414
Release Date: December 2008

This report was developed under a contract with the Small Business Administration, Office of Advocacy, and contains information and analysis that was reviewed and edited by officials of the Office of Advocacy. However, the final conclusions of the report do not necessarily reflect the views of the Office of Advocacy.

* This is an edited, reformatted and augmented version of a Small Business Research Summary, Office of Advocacy publication, dated on December 2008.

BACKGROUND

Small manufacturers are critical to the health and dynamism of U.S. manufacturing. In 2003, manufacturers with fewer than 500 employees accounted for 99 percent of all manufacturing firms and for 43 percent of all manufacturing jobs. Small manufacturers play key roles in value-chains as suppliers to larger companies, and are often the source of many product and process innovations. (For example, small firms produce 13 to 14 times more patents per employee than larger firms.) Among the many issues affecting small manufacturers, the outsourcing of manufacturing processes overseas has been one of the most widely debated, yet little researched. This paper represents a preliminary attempt at examining the role that small firms play in manufacturing and how they have been affected by trends in outsourcing of production activities.

While there are no generally accepted definitions, outsourcing refers broadly to a company's procurement of goods or services that it used to produce internally, from outside the firm. While often used interchangeably, the related term "offshoring" refers to a company's movement of such procurement to a foreign country either within or outside the firm. Offshoring is not a new phenomenon. In fact, a large fraction of the growth in world trade since the 1970s has taken the form of trade in intermediate inputs in general, and offshore outsourcing in particular. At the same time, the flip side of offshoring—the "insourcing" of activities to the United States from foreign companies—has also been increasing. Thus, it is fair to say that upon closer examination, the increasing complexity of world trade has led to a significant shift in production across industries and across the globe. This paper seeks to analyze how these trends have affected small business in the United States.

At present, little is known about the effects of outsourcing, insourcing, or offshoring on small business, or for that matter, what role small firms play in the phenomenon. This study employs two methodologies to address the issue of small business manufacturing in offshoring. First, an empirical investigation of the impact of offshoring on the performance of small manufacturers employs data on import and export activities and employment. Second, three industry case studies provide a closer and more qualitative look at how varied the impacts of offshoring can be across different industries.

Overall Findings

Offshoring, outsourcing, and insourcing do not follow any constant pattern across small firms, but rather vary greatly by industry, just as with larger firms. Results of empirical tests of changes in small firm employment do not yield significant results with respect to the effects of outsourcing, offshoring, or insourcing. The preliminary results in this paper should not be taken as the final word on how changes in the alignment of global production capacity have affected small American businesses. It would be more accurate to say that these results show that there is no simple answer to this difficult puzzle. Importantly this paper can at least lay to rest any claim that globalization is either universally detrimental or beneficial to small firms. It appears that a more accurate statement would be that both large and small firms located in the United States have benefited and suffered from outsourcing. The case studies in the second part of the paper drive home this fact.

Highlights

- While there was great variance in offshoring activity across small business industries, overall off-shoring activity grew at a greater rate in the 1990– 1997 period than in the 1998–2003 period.
- For the 1998–2003 period (the only one for which data was available), offshoring was seen as a strategic decision and not a general phenomenon. The authors determined this by noting that there was no correlation between an industry offshoring production of its product with the decisions of other industries to offshore supply of that same product as an input.
- The case studies highlight that the variance in impacts across firms and even firm size is significant with respect to outsourcing, offshoring, and insourcing. No clear patterns could be identified based on either industry or the fact that a firm was small.

SCOPE AND METHODOLOGY

The first section of the paper presents empirical results from looking at changes in small business employment in key manufacturing sectors within two time periods, 1990–1997 (using SIC codes for industry identification) and 1998–2003 (using NAICS codes for industry identification). The regression analysis relates changes in the location of production capacity to employment in small firms. The second part of the paper is a case study of three industries: apparel, auto parts, and semiconductors. These industries are not meant to be representative of a larger cross-section of small firms, but rather serve as simple illustrative examples of how outsourcing affects different industries in vastly different ways.

This report was peer reviewed consistent with the Office of Advocacy's data quality guidelines.

I. INTRODUCTION

Small manufacturers are critical to the health and dynamism of U.S. manufacturing. In 2003, manufacturers with fewer than 500 employees accounted for 99% of all manufacturing firms and for 43% of all manufacturing jobs (SBA, 2006). Small manufacturers play key roles in value-chains as suppliers to larger companies, and are often the source of many product and process innovations (e.g., small firms produce 13-14 times more patents per employee than larger firms) (CHI Research 2003). Among the many issues affecting small manufacturers, the outsourcing of manufacturing processes overseas has been one of the most widely debated, yet little researched.

While there are no generally accepted definitions, "outsourcing" refers broadly to a company's procurement of goods or services that used to be produced internally, from outside the firm. While often used interchangeably, the related term "offshoring" refers to a company's relocation of business activities to a foreign country either within or outside the firm.

Offshoring is not a new phenomenon. In fact, data suggest that a large fraction of the growth in world trade since the 1970s has taken the form of trade in intermediate inputs in general, and offshore outsourcing in particular (Feenstra 1998). Imports by U.S. multinationals from their foreign affiliates increased from 4% of their non-energy inputs in 1977 to 9% in 1997 (Council of Economic Advisers 2001). At the same time, the flip side of offshoring—the "insourcing" of activities to the United States from foreign companies—has also been increasing. Foreign direct investment in the U.S. manufacturing sector grew by $366 billion between 1990 and 2004, from $153 billion in 1990 to $519 billion in 2004 (Bureau of Economic Analysis 2006a).

Unfortunately, beyond these general facts indicating that offshoring is happening and that it seems to be intensifying, little is known about what the repercussions may be for small businesses. Related research offers only general implications for small businesses. The majority of this offshoring research does not examine firm size issues. Rather, it has focused on the impact of outsourcing and offshoring on firm and industry productivity and on how outsourcing has contributed to shifting demands for labor.[1] One study did include firm size in its survey of managers, and found that small firms are less likely to outsource (Harrison and Kelley 1993). In the business press, writers have used anecdotal evidence to suggest that outsourcing has both winners and losers among small businesses, as some small firms are caught off-guard and others are able to leverage outsourcing to compete with much larger companies (Kahn 2004).

A survey by Nexus Associates collected the views and response strategies of small manufacturers faced with global outsourcing challenges (Nexus 2005). Researchers found that while very few small manufacturers (less than 1%) had overseas manufacturing operations, nearly 10% were planning to invest in overseas manufacturing in the near future. Most small manufacturer offshoring seems to be done through sourcing and contract work with third parties, and more than half of those surveyed sourced supplies from overseas.

General theory suggests that the impact of offshoring in general on small manufacturers will depend on various factors including the competitive position of small manufacturers in their industry, what types of activities are actually being offshored, who is doing the offshoring (to what extent do small manufacturers themselves offshore activities?), and what takes offshoring's place? Unfortunately, the lack of research and data on these questions provides policymakers and advocates with little support.

The goal of this study is precisely to shed light on issues related to offshoring and the future of small manufacturers. Because of the lack of specific research on this topic, the approach we have taken is exploratory in nature—designed as much to explore broad lines of inquiry as to answer specific questions. As such, we carried out two complementary pieces of analysis: (1) an empirical investigation of the impact of offshoring on the performance of small manufacturers and (2) three industry case studies. We begin by presenting the study's hypotheses. This is followed by a brief overview of the study design and a section each on the empirical analysis and the case study research. Conclusions are drawn from both pieces of analysis in the final section.

II. Hypotheses

The overall goal of this project is to contribute to the debate about the role of offshoring in the future of small business manufacturing. Because of the lack of research on this topic, our hypotheses and approach are exploratory in nature.

Hypothesis 1: Intra-Industry Offshoring

Our first line of inquiry relates to questions of who is involved in offshoring and what type of products and processes are being offshored. The literature and available data generally indicate that large firms account for the lion's share of international trade. For example, the top 1% of trading firms had an average of 8,000 employees and accounted for a dominant 81% of trade in 2000 (Bernard, Jensen and Schott 2005). Furthermore, survey work suggests that small manufacturers are less likely to engage in outsourcing (Harrison and Kelley 1993). As a component of overall international trade, offshoring is likely to follow a similar pattern and may be even more skewed towards large firms for two reasons. First, unlike general trade, offshoring involves the integration of third parties overseas within a company's production process. This involves heightened levels of coordination and oversight of partner activities. Large companies are more likely to have the management layers available to undertake this additional coordination.

Second, firms tend to offshore large-scale activities which are well defined and not likely to change. Tailored activities, those which require rapid turnaround and high levels of customer interaction are most likely, *a priori*, to remain closer to the ultimate client (i.e., the firm doing the offshoring). These happen to be those areas of the economy where small manufacturers have comparative strengths. For example, while mass production of knock-down "Ikea"-like furniture may be easily offshored to Eastern Europe and China, these are areas of manufacturing which already tended to be dominated by large, not small manufacturers. Conversely, custom cabinetmaking, which is predominantly a small business purview, would be more likely to remain in the United States.

If this is the case, we would not expect high levels of offshoring within a given industry to be associated with poor small business performance *in that industry*. (We call this "intraindustry" offshoring.) Large manufacturers would account for the majority of that offshoring and may be streamlining their workforces and reducing their domestic value-added, but small manufacturers would continue to serve different niches within the market.

Hypothesis 2: Related Industry Offshoring

Next, we explore two issues connected to the impact of "related" manufacturing activity offshoring and its impact on small manufacturers: (1) the impact of offshoring of "upstream" design operations, and (2) the impact of other industries' offshoring decisions. Outsourcing in manufacturing has been moving from the outsourcing of core manufacturing production processes to product engineering and design. For example, Motorola stopped producing cell phones in the United States some time ago, but it maintained design and engineering in-house and on-shore. This is no longer the case, as evidenced by the proposed $30 billion MotorolaFlextronics deal in 2000 for Flextronics to build a range of components and complete final products for Motorola, including cell phones (CNN Money 2005). Contract manufacturers such as Flextronics are increasingly engaging in product design and operations for their clients in the United States.[2]

There is evidence that compelled by original equipment manufacturers' (OEMs) increasing demand on their suppliers to meet higher quality and delivery benchmarks, many small manufacturers have moved up the value chain and, consequently, boosted their productivity (Luria 2002). For those sectors where small manufacturers provide high-end products and services to OEMs and participate in joint design and development of products, OEMs tend to be selective in building supplier relationships. Changing the supplier base in these cases is associated with high costs of re-sourcing (Whitford and Zeitlin 2003). It is intuitive then, that if the OEM moves upstream activities such as design and development offshore, small manufacturers plugged into that supply chain will be negatively affected.

Offshoring of these high-end design and other services would be likely to have a more profound, long-term negative impact on small business manufacturers than intra-industry offshoring of core production activities. As engineering and design services move overseas, foreign suppliers have the advantage, plugging into supply chains being formed around these upstream activities and services being provided. For example, as Hewlett-Packard has built up its research and development (R&D) centers throughout Asia, more and more manufacturing and related sourcing has moved to the region.[3] Therefore, in industries where there are indications that these upstream activities are being offshored, we would expect to see a negative impact on small businesses.[4]

Similarly, small manufacturers are affected not only by offshoring in their own industry, but by sourcing decisions in other industries. For example, the automobile industry's decision to source parts from abroad would be expected to affect the domestic auto parts industry.

Hypothesis 3: Insourcing

Finally, we turn to the impact of "insourcing"—foreign companies locating their plants and operation in the United States—on small U.S. manufacturers. The United States is one of the world's largest recipients of foreign direct investment (FDI), and FDI stocks in manufacturing grew by $366 billion between 1990 and 2004, from $153 billion in 1990 to $519 billion in 2004 (Bureau of Economic Analysis 2006a). Toyota, Honda, and other auto manufacturers have increasingly established manufacturing plants in the United States with significant levels of local purchasing, some of it for small manufacturers.[5] Other foreign manufacturers, especially those in the information technology and life sciences areas, are establishing R&D centers in the United States. This "insourcing" by foreign companies clearly creates opportunities for domestic small manufacturers.

However, the competitive pressures guiding outsourcing by U.S. companies are similar to those faced by foreign companies (though certain regulatory factors may affect decisions in some industries). Therefore, one would expect insourcing not to offset the impacts of offshoring as it would occur in different industry segments or be of a different type. In other words, if a certain U.S. industry segment is offshoring assembly operations, this is an indication that overseas assemblers have a competitive advantage in this manufacturing activity and FDI is unlikely to be destined to the establishment of U.S. assembly operations. Therefore, we expect that, while insourcing or onshoring does create opportunities for small manufacturers overall, these are not likely to mitigate the impacts of offshoring for small manufacturers in specific industries.

To summarize, our hypotheses are:

1) *Intra-industry offshoring* – Within any individual industry segment (e.g., automobile parts, electronics, apparel), an industry's offshoring does not, in the short term, negatively affect small manufacturers.
2) *Other-industry offshoring & upstream activities* – Offshoring "upstream" and "downstream" of an industry segment has a negative impact on small businesses. Upstream activities refers to portions of the value chain, such as design and engineering services, that are related and provide inputs into a core manufacturing process. "Downstream" refers to those segments of the economy which purchase or use the outputs of a given industry.
3) *Insourcing* – Foreign investment in manufacturing in the United States is concentrated in industry segments and activities where there is little corresponding offshoring. As such, while insourcing creates opportunities for small manufacturers, they are in areas different than those affected by offshoring.

III. Overview of the Research Design

We undertook two complementary lines of investigation to examine the impact of offshoring on small business manufacturing: (1) an empirical examination of how offshoring explains differences in small business performance across industries and (2) three industry case studies. This combination of approaches allowed us to study broad cross-industry factors affecting small businesses as well as to undertake more nuanced and in-depth investigation of how offshoring has affected three industries. We believe these two approaches are complementary and appropriate given the exploratory nature of the questions at hand. Table 1 summarizes how each hypothesis was assessed through this combined approach.

Table 1. Summary of Research Approach

Hypotheses	Empirical Analysis • Multi-step regression on industry outsourcing and small business performance	Case Studies • Three industry case studies – electronics, automotive, and apparel • 3 firm-level examples per industry case • Review of secondary case studies and other sources
Hypothesis 1: Intra-industry offshoring	• Data: intra-industry offshoring proxied with industry purchases of imported intermediates (own +extra)	• Identify extent to which small manufacturers have been affected by offshoring within their industry segment • Explore perceptions on the costs and benefits of offshoring strategies within the industry
Hypothesis 2: Related industry offshoring	• Data: related-industry and other- industry offshoring proxied by industry intermediate imports.	• Explore types of activities being offshored by industry suppliers and users, and impact on small businesses
Hypothesis 3: Insourcing	• Data: foreign direct investment by industry	• Investigate extent to which small businesses in industry have received supply contracts with foreign companies locating in U.S. • Examine types of activities being insourced by foreign firms

These two pieces of the study are presented in the sections that follow.

IV. Empirical Analysis

Model

Our empirical investigation attempts to explain industry-level differences in small business performance by levels and changes in offshoring, insourcing and differing industry characteristics. Our general model relates changes in small business performance between two time periods in an industry to intra-industry offshoring (hypothesis #1), offshoring in other industries (hypothesis #2), insourcing (hypothesis #3), and industry characteristics.

ΔS_i=F(I_i, ΔOi_i, ΔOr_i, ΔOo_i, FDI_i, Z_i)

Where:

ΔS_i = Change in employment in small firms in industry i between the two periods;

I_i = Overall performance of industry i between the two periods;

ΔOi_i = Change in industry offshoring industry i between the two periods

ΔOe_i = Change in the offshoring in industries *related* to industry i between the two periods (extra-industry outsourcing)

ΔOo_i = Change in other-industry outsourcing intensity of industry i's products between the two periods (other-industry outsourcing)

FDIi = Foreign direct investment in industry i (a measure of insourcing)

Zi = Industry characteristics

Data and Measurement Issues

We assembled two similar, yet distinct sets of data: one for the period 1990-1997 based on the Standard Industrial Classification (SIC) system, and another covering 1998-2003 based on the newer North American Industrial Classification System (NAICS). Both contain the same variables with data from the same basic sources, but the fundamental shift around 1997 in the industry classification system used by American statistical offices for industry data significantly affected manufacturing industries, rendering data from the two periods incomparable.[6] Concordances to move between SIC and NAICS data do exist. However, these are reliable for statistical purposes in just a handful of manufacturing industries. This raises the risk that industry changes in the resulting data would be due to classification changes rather than underlying changes in the performance of small manufacturers, offshoring patterns, etc. Though combining the data across the 1997 change would create a much longer time series for the analysis (1990- 2003), doing so was not judged to be worth the risks. Instead, we decided to keep the two sets of data separate, providing two snapshots of analysis.

The remainder of this section describes each data element and estimations. Except where noted, two data points are collected for each time period corresponding to the initial and ending year (1990 and 1997 for SIC data, and 1998 and 2003 for NAICS). (A more detailed description of the data and estimations is provided in Appendix A.)

Small Business Performance

We look at changes in employment in each industry among firms with less than 500 and less than 20 employees. As small businesses would tend to follow overall industry trends, we also look at overall industry performance and changes in employment among all firms as a control.

Offshoring

We use two estimates for offshoring. The first approach uses a technique used by Feenstra and Hanson (1996) to estimate industry purchases of imported manufactured intermediate inputs. This is constructed by combining detailed trade data from the International Trade Commission and input-output tables from the Bureau of Labor Statistics[7] indicating the value of intermediate inputs that each industry purchases from every other industry. Each industry's offshoring is estimated as the sum of the industry's input purchases from each other industry multiplied by the import penetration of that industry.

We further separate offshoring into three components: intra-industry offshoring (Oii), extra-industry offshoring (Oei) and other industry offshoring (Ooi). Intra-industry offshoring looks only at an industry's imported intermediate purchases of products it produces (e.g. the computer and office equipment industry's purchase of imported computer and office equipment). Extra-industry offshoring refers to an industry's purchase of imported intermediates from *other* industries. An example of extra-industry offshoring is the computer industry's purchase of electrical equipment and plastics. Other-industry offshoring looks at the estimated offshoring of other industries of the products an industry produces. Because detailed input-output tables were not available for all years, this method is used only for the NAICS-based calculations of 1998- 2003.

The second source for industry offshoring also proxies offshoring by looking at intermediate manufacturing imports at the industry level, but is constructed through a different process. Peter Schott developed a set of estimates at the four-digit SIC level (1987 revision) from 1972 to 2001 where intermediate imports are defined as the sum of product-level imports categories that contain variants of the word "part" (Schott 2004). The difference between these two approaches is that the first uses input-output data to estimate offshoring at the industry level, whereas the second uses details of product import descriptions.

Dollar levels of offshoring vary widely across industries, reflecting both the scale of different industries as well as the intensity of offshoring. To account for these differences, we look at offshoring intensity, or dollar values of offshoring as a share of industry shipments as well as the change over time.

Insourcing

As a proxy for insourcing, we look at foreign direct investment inflows by industry, specifically changes in the stock of FDI between time periods. Again, as scale matters in determining the impact of insourcing on performance, we look at changes in FDI stocks between the beginning and end years divided by total industry shipments.

Industry Characteristics

We use an employment by occupation approach to measure industry orientation towards innovation and technology, production, and sales. This general approach has been used often in past research to measure the technology-orientation of industries and regions, and more recently, it has been used to measure issues such as the production-orientation of industries.[8] Rather than looking at "output" issues such as patents and other technology measures of innovation, an employment approach looks at how concentrated employment in an industry is in certain technology, or other functional occupations. For example, an industry with a high concentration of scientists is presumed to be more science-focused than one whose employees are mostly machinists. For each industry, we look at the share of industry employment in three sets of occupations: creative, science and technology; sales and related; and production.

Findings

The dataset developed for this project has 458 records (N = 458) for the period of analysis 1990-1997 (corresponding to 4-digit SIC level) and 84 records (N = 84) for the period 1998-2003 (4-digit NAICS level). For each of these time periods, we analyzed two sets of small businesses: small manufacturers with less than 500 employees and very small manufacturers with less than 20 employees. Analysis points to distinct performance differences between these two groups.

Overall Small Business Performance

Small manufacturers' performance varied widely among manufacturing industries. For example between 1990 and 1997, in the case of small manufacturers with less than 500 employees, the "malt beverages" industry (SIC 2082) experienced the highest employment growth (260%), whereas the "hard surface floor coverings" industry (SIC 3996) experienced the highest percentage point decline (-88%). During the same period, the performance of very small manufacturers also differed widely with the "paper – laminated and coated packaging" industry (SIC 2671) growing the fastest (over 980% employment growth) and the "petroleum refining" industry (SIC 2911) shrinking by 69%.

Similar wide variations in change in employment for small and very small manufacturers were observed in the 1998-2003 period. For firms with less than 500 employees, the "iron and steel mills ferroalloy manufacturing" industry had the highest employment growth (80%), whereas the "footwear manufacturing" industry (NAICS 3162) experienced the highest percentage point decline (-56%). The "iron and steel mills ferroalloy manufacturing" industry also was the fastest growing industry (growth of 370%) with regard to very small firm employment. The "apparel accessories and other apparel manufacturing" industry (NAICS 3159) had the highest percentage point decline (-48%).

As expected, employment performance in an industry overall is positively correlated with changes among large (over 500 employees) companies, small firms, and very small firms for both time periods. However, this relationship is the strongest for large firms, and the weakest for the very small, suggesting that something different is happening to small (and especially very small) firms. (See correlation matrices below and figures in Appendix B.[9]) Our hypotheses are that a portion of these differences in performance could stem from a combination of differences in offshoring and insourcing in each industry.

Patterns in Offshoring

Levels and changes in offshoring intensity varied from industry to industry during both periods of analysis. Offshoring intensity increased by over 80% from 1990-1997 in the "furniture and fixtures" industry (SIC 2599). The biggest decline in offshoring intensity occurred in the "dolls manufacturing" industry (SIC 3942). The rate of highest growth in offshoring intensity decreased in the subsequent period of analysis, with the highest growth (just above 5%) in offshore intensity observed in the "leather and hide tanning and finishing" industry (NAICS 3161). Contrary to common perception, the "computer and peripheral equipment manufacturing" industry witnessed the greatest decline (over 13%) in offshoring intensity between 1998 and 2003.

Correlations Matrix 1				
Variables	**SIC-based 4-digit data for the period 1990-1997**			
Percentage change in employment for all firms in industry	1.000			
Percentage change in employment for firms with less than 20 employees	0.290	1.000		
Percentage change in employment for firms with less than 500 employees	0.597**	0.467**	1.000	
Percentage change in employment for firms with over 500 employees	0.850**	0.071	0.315**	1.000
**** Correlation is significant at the 0.01 level**				

Correlations Matrix 2				
Variables	**NAICS-based 4-digit data for the period 1998-2003**			
Percentage change in employment for all firms in industry	1.000			
Percentage change in employment for firms with less than 20 employees	0.114	1.000		
Percentage change in employment for firms with less than 500 employees	0.613**	0.660**	1.000	
Percentage change in employment for firms with over 500 employees	0.940**	0.060	0.456**	1.000
**** Correlation is significant at the 0.01 level**				

Correlations Matrix 3					
Variables	**SIC-based 4-digit data for the period 1990-1997**				
Change in insourcing	1.000				
Change in outsourcing	-0.044	1.000			
Outsourcing intensity	-0.040	0.555**	1.000		
Import intensity	-0.051	0.025	0.191**	1.000	
Change in import intensity	-0.034	0.051	0.295**	.663**	1.000
** Correlation is significant at the 0.01 level					

Between 1990 and 1997, levels of offshoring exhibited a moderately strong positive correlation (r = 0.555) with changes in offshoring. In other words, offshoring over the period tended to grow faster in industries with higher offshoring levels to begin with. This trend reversed itself for the 1998-2003 period, when changes in offshoring were negatively correlated (r = -0.288) with levels in 1998. One potential explanation of this is that industries with matured offshoring portfolios had less incentive and scope for further offshoring.

As described earlier, we were able to separate offshoring for the 1998-2003 period into three components: intra-industry offshoring, extra-industry offshoring, and other-industry offshoring. It is interesting to note the distinctions in patterns in these three components of offshoring. First, industries with high degrees of intra-industry offshoring did not necessarily have high levels of extra-industry offshoring. Second, industries with high degrees of intraindustry offshoring were not necessarily the ones that other industries offshored heavily. These observations imply that in most cases offshoring by any industry was strategic—no specific industry's products were offshored by all other industries to a similar degree. The charts presented in Appendix B show the variations across industries in intra-industry, extra-industry and other-industry offshoring.

Between 1998 and 2003, intra-industry offshoring as measured by the change in offshoring within own industry had negative correlation with other-industry offshoring (r = -0.443, significant at 0.01 level) as measured by the change in other industries' offshoring of the industry's products.

Correlations Matrix 4					
Variables	**NAICS-based data for the period 1998-2003**				
Change in insourcing	1.000				
Outsourcing intensity	-0.155	1.000			
Change in intra-industry outsourcing	0.029	-0.234*	1.000		
Change in extra-industry outsourcing	0.092	-0.207	0.262*	1.000	
Change in other-industry outsourcing	0.059	0.262	-0.443**	-0.172	1.000
* Correlation is significant at the 0.05 level; ** Correlation is significant at the 0.01 level					

Patterns in Insourcing

The stock of foreign direct investment (FDI) in U.S. manufacturing grew from $152 billion in 1987 to $270 billion in 1997 and $492 billion in 2003.[10] Despite this consistent macro trend, insourcing has varied across industries and over time. For the 1990 to 1997 period, the intensity of insourcing, measured by FDI inflow divided by total shipments, ranged from 147% in "miscellaneous publishing" (SIC 274) to negative 10% in grain mill products (SIC 204). (A negative value indicates a fall in the FDI stock.) For the 1998 to 2003 period, variations in insourcing between manufacturing industry segments diminished, ranging from a high of 39% in "soap, cleaning compound and toilet preparation products" industry to a decline of 11% in "communications equipment manufacturing."

Of particular relevance to our hypothesis on insourcing, levels and changes in offshoring tended to be negatively associated with insourcing between 1990 and 1997.[11] In other words, insourcing tends to happen in industries with lower levels of offshoring and where offshoring is not growing. In the subsequent period of analysis, the pattern remained the same, though correlations are not statistically significant.

Regression Analyses

We developed two sets of multivariate regression models, each using ordinary least square (OLS) techniques for small manufacturers with less than 500 employees and for very small firms with less than 20 employees. First, we analyzed the SIC-based data for the 1990-97 period, and then applied the multi-step models for the later period 1998-2003 using NAICSbased data.[12] Results of the regression tests are presented below.

The first model presents the combined effects of three primary independent variables— (1) change in insourcing between 1990 and 1997, (2) change in offshoring between 1990 and 1997, and (3) offshoring intensity in 1990—on the dependent variable (percentage change in employment of very small firms with less than 20 employees). The test is marginally significant and the variables collectively explain only 3.2% of variation in change in employment. In this model, change in insourcing and change in offshoring turn out to be statistically significant predictors of change in employment in very small firms. In the case of change in offshoring (B = -1.106, significant at the 0.05 level), the negative sign of the coefficient indicates that increases in offshoring are associated with decreases in employment. In contrast, the positive sign of the effect of insourcing (B=0.465, significant at the 0.05 level) implies that insourcing is associated with gains in small manufacturer employment, consistent with our hypotheses.

In the second step, we test the combined effects of variables representing the industry's employment characteristics in addition to the insourcing and offshoring variables. While two of the industry characteristics variables (percentage employed in high-tech occupations and percentage employed in production occupations) are marginally significant, insourcing and offshoring coefficients retain their significance and change somewhat in their magnitude.[13] The overall test has a weaker significance and the variables collectively explain only 4.4% of the industry variation observed in change in employment in very small firms.

In the third step, we test the combined effects of all the variables in Model 2 in the presence of the overall change in employment in the industry. The explanatory power of the model increases significantly with the addition of this variable, indicating the close relationship of the overall employment trends in the industry and changes in employment for small firms as discussed earlier.[14] Yet more importantly, when the effects of the overall employment trends in the industry are controlled for, the influences of insourcing, offshoring (significant at 0.01 level) and industry characteristics on change in small business employment become stronger than before. This model shows that industries with larger increases in offshoring have larger declines in employment among very small firms. Although marginally significant, change in insourcing has a positive effect on change in employment for very small firms.

Next, we test the aforementioned three models for firms with less than 500 employees. While the regression results are self explanatory, two important points emerge that merit further discussion. First, Model 1 and Model 2 fail to hold statistical significance, while Model 3, which controls for the change in overall employment is marginally significant, making the results of the tests suggestive rather than definitive. Keeping in mind the suggestive nature of these results, it is still interesting to note that changes in offshoring continue to have a negative, marginally significant effect on changes in employment.

Regression Analysis on SIC Data Relating to Period 1990-1997												
	Firms with less than 20 employees						Firms with less than 500 employees					
	Model 1		Model 2		Model 3		Model 1		Model 2		Model 3	
Independent Variable	Unstandardized Coefficient		Unstandardized Coefficient		Unstandardized Coefficient		Unstandardized Coefficient		Unstandardized Coefficient		Unstandardized Coefficient	
Change in Insourcing	0.465	**	0.661	**	0.485	***	0.223		0.012		-0.209	
Outsourcing Intensity	0.591		0.744		0.883	***	0.234		0.136		0.301	
Change in Outsourcing	-1.106	**	-1.166	**	-1.237	*	-0.495		-0.479		-0.594	***
Percentage Employment in High-Tech Occupations			2.318	***	2.764	**			-1.095		-0.264	
Percentage Employment in Sales Occupations			2.622		3.258				-0.127		0.726	
Percentage Employment in Production Occupations			1.465	***	1.653	**			-0.759		-0.384	
Percentage Change in Employment for All Firms					0.51	*					0.765	*

Regression Analysis (Continued)

Regression Analysis on SIC Data Relating to Period 1990-1997												
	Firms with less than 20 employees						Firms with less than 500 employees					
	Model 1		Model 2		Model 3		Model 1		Model 2		Model 3	
Constant	0.196	**	-1.05		-1.225	***	0.035	***	0.642		0.32	
R-Square	0.032		0.045		0.116		0.010		0.025		0.305	
*** Significant at 0.1 level, ** Significant at 0.05 level, * Significant at 0.01 level												
Dependent Variable: Percentage change in employment												

Regression Analysis on NAICS Data Relating to Period 1998-2003												
	Firms with less than 20 employees						Firms with less than 500 employees					
	Model 1		Model 2		Model 3		Model 1		Model 2		Model 3	
Independent Variable	Unstandardized Coefficient		Unstandardized Coefficient		Unstandardized Coefficient		Unstandardized Coefficient		Unstandardized Coefficient		Unstandardized Coefficient	
Change in Insourcing	0.022		-0.144		-0.199		0.101		0.039		-0.041	
Outsourcing Intensity	-0.179		4.658		5.18		-1.374	**	0.745		1.499	
Change in Intra-industry	0.242		8.14		6.408		-0.970		3.999		1.497	
Change in Extra-industry	1.961		1.944		0.115		3.382	**	3.249		0.607	

Regression Analysis on NAICS Data Relating to Period 1998-2003												
	Firms with less than 20 employees						Firms with less than 500 employees					
	Model 1		Model 2		Model 3		Model 1		Model 2		Model 3	
Change in Other-industry Outsourcing	-8.756	*	-12.866	*	-12.66	*	-0.443		-1.771	***	-1.473	
Percentage Employment in High-Tech Occupations			-2.64	**	-2.468	***			-0.872	***	-0.624	
Percentage Employment in Sales Occupations			-5.855		-5.693				-2.355	***	-2.121	
Percentage Employment in Production Occupations			-1.56	***	-1.398				-0.864	*	-0.631	
Percentage change in employment for all firms in the industry					0.475						0.686	**
Constant	0.051		1.004	***	0.943	***	-0.003		0.478	**	0.39	**
R-Square	0.146		0.319		0.324		0.150		0.236		0.325	
* Significant at 0.1 level, ** Significant at 0.01 level												
Dependent Variable: Percentage change in employment												

Next we turn to the NAICS-based data for the 1998-2003 period. The first model for firms with less than 20 employees tests the combined effects on change in employment of insourcing, offshoring intensity and three variables representing changes in offshoring. The overall test is significant, and collectively these variables explain 14.6% of variation in change in employment. Only one independent variable—change in other industries' offshoring of the industry's products—is significant with a negative effect ($B = -8.756$, $p = 0.001$), implying that an increase in other-industry offshoring negatively affects very small firm employment. However, neither change in offshoring of own-industry products nor change in an industry's offshoring of products produced by other industries has any statistically significant effect on change in employment. In subsequent tests (Model 2 and Model 3), the strength of the effect of change in other-industry offshoring increases. The concluding model shows a substantial negative effect of this variable which is statistically significant. Although marginally significant, the high-tech employment variable indicates that during 1998-2003, industries that had a higher percentage of high-tech jobs witnessed lower employment growth within very small firms.

We also tested these models for firms with less than 500 employees. The degree of influence and the statistical significance of predictors change from model to model, with the overall tests failing to retain significance. The general failure of the model to test the effects of the variables on NAICS data makes the regression analysis for the period 1998-2003 largely inconclusive. However, the general direction of the effect of change in other-industry offshoring remained negative all through.

Summary Findings from the Empirical Analyses

Although the empirical analysis is not definitive, the findings nevertheless are suggestive of a of number issues pertaining to offshoring and the performance of small manufacturers. These are discussed in relation to each of our original hypotheses.

Hypothesis 1: Intra-Industry Offshoring

Contrary to our hypothesis, offshoring seems to have a negative impact on small business performance. Analysis of the SIC data reveals that for very small firms, this negative effect of offshoring persisted while controlling for the influence of other industry characteristics and overall employment trends.

Offshoring also had a negative effect on employment growth of small firms (with less than 500 employees), although the strength of the effect was weaker than that for very small firms. It is important to note, however, that there is a potential endogeneity problem in that declining industries may be both more likely to outsource and more likely to lose employment.

Hypothesis 2: Other-Industry Offshoring and Upstream Activities

When offshoring is separated into its intra-industry, extra-industry, and other-industry components, intra-industry offshoring turns out to be less important than other-industry offshoring in predicting small business employment performance. For very small firms, changes in the level of other industries' offshoring of an industry's products has a significant negative impact on very small firms in that industry. This impact is stronger than the effects of the industry's own offshoring activity (offshoring of own activities or offshoring of products produced by other industries). This finding supports our hypothesis that when related industries offshore, they adversely affect the performance of small businesses in the core industry. We were unable to empirically examine issues related to the offshoring of upstream design activities.

Hypothesis 3: Insourcing

The data is inconclusive regarding the relationship between insourcing and offshoring. Between 1990 and 1997, correlation tests indicate that insourcing was negatively associated with offshoring levels and changes. For the 1998-03 period, this negative relationship was maintained with respect to levels of offshoring. However, for this period, insourcing shows a positive association with changes in offshoring. Given that the correlation coefficients are insignificant for both the SIC-based data and for the NAICS-based data, the general direction of association between insourcing and offshoring can only be construed to be suggestive.

V. CASE STUDIES

To complement the empirical research, we carried out three industry case studies to provide a more complete picture of offshoring and small business perspectives not otherwise captured by the limited hard data on offshoring. These case studies allow us to identify, in a qualitative way: (1) the extent to which small manufacturers have lost markets because of offshoring, (2) the types of activities being offshored by industry and the impact on small businesses, and (3) the extent to which small businesses in manufacturing industries have benefited from insourcing through supply contracts with foreign companies in the United States and abroad. In addition, we were interested in exploring how available data on offshoring corresponded to the perceptions and views of industry participants. In other words, given the limitations of the data discussed above, we wanted to ascertain how representative of industry activity the available data are.

Case Study Methodology

Three industry cases were selected using four broad criteria: (1) changes in offshoring, (2) the relative importance of small businesses in a particular industry (size and share of employment and number of small firms in the industry), (3) the availability of secondary data, and (4) the importance of the sector to the future competitive landscape of the country.

We are interested in examining industry segments that have experienced large shifts towards offshoring, either in the past or present. As mentioned previously, offshoring is not a new phenomenon, and different manufacturing industries have been transformed through offshoring over the years. We wanted to look at industries at various degrees of "maturity" in the offshoring process in order to highlight different issues that may be prevalent at different stages.

Second, as this study is specifically concerned with small manufacturers, we are interested in industries that are important to small manufacturers. Manufacturing industries vary by small business intensity and overall size of the industry, so that the number of people employed in small manufacturing firms ranges from a low of 22,365 in petroleum and coal products in 2003 to a high of just over 1 million in fabricated metal products (SBA 2006). In nearly all cases, the variety in industries within these broad industry segments is greater than differences between them. For example, while about 30% of all employees in the computer and electronics industry are employed by small manufacturers, the small business share of sub-industries ranges from 7% in search, detection and guidance instruments (NAICS 334511) to 74% in electronic coil, transformer, and other inductor manufacturing (NAICS 334416).

Third, as we intend to build as much as possible on secondary source materials, we are somewhat restricted in the selection of industry segments by those that are popular with analysts and researchers. Offshoring in industries such as computers and electronics and the automotive industry are relatively well researched, for example, compared to the paper or wood products industry.

Lastly, different manufacturing industry segments are more or less important to future economic growth and prosperity in the country. Therefore, we wanted to examine sectors that are broadly seen as critical to future competitiveness and that have promising global growth prospects. Looking at the period 1987 and 2001, nearly all of the growth in manufacturing real GDP was due to growth in motor vehicles, parts and industrial equipment, and electronic and other electric equipment.[15] Other sectors were broadly stable, or declining in the case of printing and publishing, leather products, and tobacco.

Looking across our four criteria, we selected three broad industries: apparel, auto parts, and semiconductors. These three industries account for over 400,000 jobs in small manufacturing firms in 2003 as follows: 220,508 jobs in apparel (NAICS 315), 139,027 in auto parts (NAICS 3363), and 22,613 in semiconductors (NAICS 334413) (SBA 2006). They have varying levels of technological sophistication, and they have varying small business intensities (both between industries and among their sub-industries).

The case studies draw upon two main sources of information: secondary sources and firm-level cases conducted by the study team. Nine firm-level cases of small manufacturers, three in each industry, were carried out to inform the research through qualitative, contextual information. Semi-structured interview techniques were used, and firms are not identified by name to preserve the confidentiality of participating firms.

Case 1: Apparel

The design and production of apparel (i.e., clothing) is one of the oldest manufacturing industries in the world and one in which the production process is truly global. Apparel is a textbook example of a labor-intensive industry in which one can see the clear migration of production from industrialized countries to lower-cost developing countries over the last century. As recently as 1973, U.S. textile and apparel industries employed 2.4 million people, 1.0 million in textiles and 1.4 million in apparel (Bureau of Labor Statistics 2006). By 2005, the situation had changed dramatically with 260,200 apparel jobs (NAICS 315) and 217,900 textile jobs (NAICS 313), approximately 3.4% of total U.S. manufacturing sector employment. Offshoring has and continues to play a large role in this transformation. This study focuses on the apparel industry because of its historic dominance by small manufacturers and the growing significance of very small U.S. firms as a share of overall employment and total apparel establishments.

Overview of Industry

Apparel firms are concerned with turning raw textiles, or fabrics, into clothing of various types (Figure 1).[16] This involves several modular activities: design, pattern creation, fabric dying, washing, spreading, cutting, sewing and assembly, pressing, etc. Despite the advent of the sewing machine in the mid-1880s and mechanization of washing, cutting, and pressing, the sewing and assembly stage of apparel production remains labor-intensive with few economies of scale. By contrast, the process of textile production allows for significant economies of scale and automation. Therefore, the textile industry has tended to be dominated by larger companies while apparel manufacturing has involved considerably more small firms.

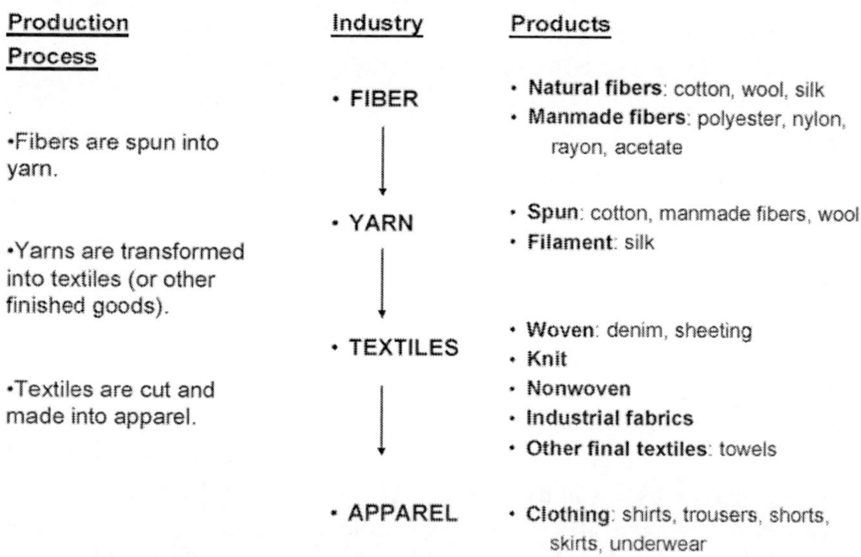

Source: U.S. International Trade Commission (2004).

Figure 1. Schematic of Fiber, Textile and Apparel Industry Production.

After growing from 1950-1973, U.S. apparel manufacturing employment has been in steady decline for over three decades (Figure 2). The total number of jobs reached a record low of 260,200 in 2005 from a high of 1.4 million apparel jobs in 1973. There is no sign of abatement in this trend. Analysts point to three main reasons for the rapid demise of the apparel industry in employment terms: (1) the rise of buyer-driven production; (2) information technology advances that allow increased data sharing, real-time connectivity between producers and retailers, and leaner manufacturing; and (3) increasing loss of market share to imports.[17]

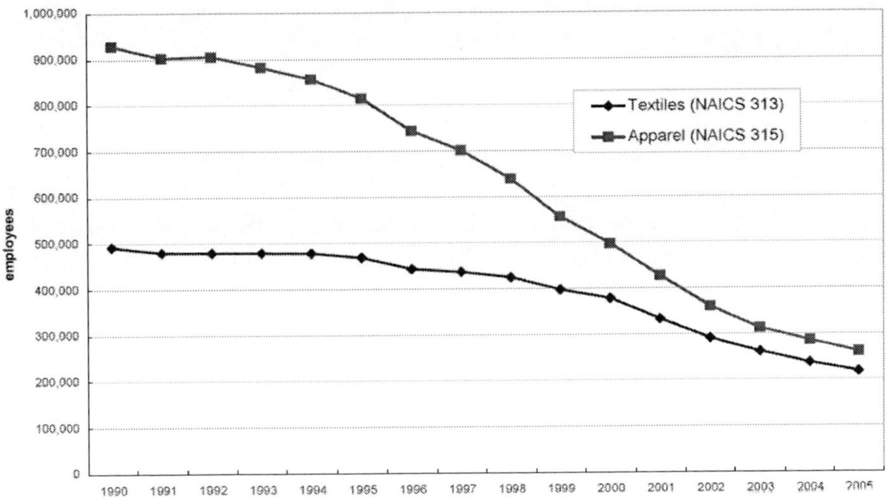

Source: U.S. Department of Labor, Bureau of Labor Statistics, Current Employment Statistics, http://www.bls.gov/ces/#data.

Figure 2. Apparel and Textile Industry Employment, 1990-2005.

Buyer-Driven Production

Unlike the post-war period when large apparel manufacturers dictated fashion and production runs, retailers have come to the fore over the past few decades. Across the board, a variety of retailers—from mass merchandisers, like Wal-Mart, to department stores, like Macy's, and national specialty chains, like the Gap—are exerting tremendous pressure on apparel manufacturers. Not only do these retailers play a lead role in design, but they have also increased their margins by exacting lower garment prices from producers and shifting greater inventory management responsibilities to them. Technological advances (discussed in the next section), especially IT-enabled advances in supply chain management, have aided large retailers in their move to become leaner and more price competitive. The impact of this buyer-driven revolution is twofold: (1) price pressures have hastened the rapid erosion of U.S apparel manufacturers' competitiveness vis-à-vis foreign suppliers since the 1970s, and (2) large apparel manufacturers both domestically and overseas have made themselves indispensable to retailers. With their ability to invest in the requisite IT and supply chain management infrastructure, they are able to provide retailers with full-package solutions of production, distribution and inventory management desired by retailers.

Technological Change

On the manufacturing side, computer-aided design (CAD) systems have introduced efficiencies in the apparel production process, but technological advances in supply chain management—e.g., digital bar coding and electronic data interchange (EDI) of point-of-sales data—are having even larger impacts on the industry. The adoption of EDI and other related technologies has allowed large retailers and their suppliers to reduce production response times and shift inventory management burdens from retailers to manufacturers. This industry evolution has tended to benefit the larger apparel manufacturers because of the significant capital investment required. A 2005 UNCTAD study found that large East Asian multinational apparel manufacturers, in concert with large multinational apparel retailers in the United States, Europe and Japan, are increasingly determining the direction of apparel manufacturing FDI and the location of apparel production facilities globally (UNCTAD 2005, 27). The UNCTAD study further predicts greater consolidation of apparel production in larger factories and in a smaller number of locations in the period following the expiration of the Multifiber Agreement. This view has been echoed by U.S. trade organizations, such as the American Apparel and Footwear Association.[18]

Loss of Market Share to Imports

In the last 15 years, U.S. apparel imports have more than tripled from \$21.9 billion in 1990 to \$68.7 billion in 2005. U.S. apparel exports have also risen during this period, but from a comparatively modest \$2.2 billion to \$4.5 billion (OTEXA 2006). Whereas today's industrialized countries dominated global apparel exports in the 1960s, today, developing countries produce nearly three-quarters of the world's apparel exports (UNCTAD 2005). As a labor-intensive, assembly-based industry, there is little surprise that apparel production has shifted to lower cost countries. Despite the 1974 Multi-Fiber Arrangement, a bilateral system of quotas intended to protect the U.S. apparel industry, apparel imports to the U.S. have continued to rise over the past three decades. The American Apparel Manufacturers Association (now American Apparel and Footwear Association) estimated that imports' share of the domestic market grew from less than 10% before 1970 to over 50% by the mid-1990s (Doeringer and Watson 1999).

Table 2. Top 10 Apparel Supplying Countries and Regions to U.S. Market, 1990-2005

1990 rank (% of total)	1995 rank (% of total)	2000 rank (% of total)	2005 rank (% of total)
Hong Kong (16.5)	CBI countries (15.7)	CBI countries (16.7)	China (22.0)
China (12.5)	CAFTA countries (13.7)	CAFTA countries (15.7)	CBI countries (14.0)
Taiwan (10.6)	Hong Kong (12.1)	Mexico (14.7)	CAFTA countries (13.2)
South Korea (9.8)	China (10.2)	China (7.9)	Mexico (8.8)
CBI countries (8.9)	Mexico (7.4)	Hong Kong (7.8)	Hong Kong (5.1)
CAFTA countries (6.5)	Taiwan (5.9)	Dominican Republic (4.2)	India (4.3)
Philippines (4.7)	Dominican Republic (5.0)	Honduras (4.1)	Indonesia (4.2)
Italy (3.2)	South Korea (4.7)	South Korea (4.0)	Vietnam (4.0)
Dominican Republic (3.2)	Philippines (4.4)	Bangladesh (3.7)	Honduras (3.8)
Indonesia (2.9)	Indonesia (3.4)	Taiwan (3.6)	Bangladesh (3.5)
$21.9 billion	$34.6 billion	$57.2 billion	$68.7 billion

Notes: The Caribbean Basin Initiative (CBI) countries refer to the 23 countries of Antigua and Barbuda, Aruba, Bahamas, Barbados, Belize, British Virgin Islands, Costa Rica, Dominica, Dominican Republic, El Salvador, Grenada, Guatemala, Guyana, Haiti, Honduras, Jamaica, Montserrat, Netherlands Antilles, Nicaragua, Panama, St. Kitts and Nevis, St. Lucia, St. Vincent and the Grenadines, and Trinidad and Tobago.

The Central American Free Trade Agreement (CAFTA) countries refer to the five countries of Costa Rica, El Salvador, Guatemala, Honduras, Nicaragua, and since 2004, the Dominican Republic.

Source: Office for Textiles and Apparel (OTEXA), International Trade Administration, U.S. Department of Commerce.

Offshoring in the Industry

Offshoring has long been a characteristic of the apparel industry, first in the outsourcing to third-party domestic manufacturers and then to foreign contract manufacturers. Doeringer and Watson point out that since mass production began, apparel production has been divided amongst: (1) apparel manufacturers, (2) contractors, and (3) intermediaries (or "jobbers") (Doeringer and Watson 1999). Manufacturers design clothing, purchase inputs, produce apparel in their own facilities, and market them to retailers. Intermediaries—the global retailers and buyers of today—design clothing, purchase and cut fabric, ship the fabric to contractors for assembly, and market the finished apparel to retailers. In the 1950s and 1960s, most outsourcing of production went to U.S. contractors.

However, as in other manufacturing sectors, recent decades have witnessed significant growth in the use of offshore suppliers. For example, Carter's, Inc., the largest branded manufacturer and marketer of apparel exclusively for babies and young children, went from owning multiple U.S. sewing, textile and related facilities and five overseas sewing facilities in 1999 to zero apparel manufacturing facilities, domestically or abroad, in 2006 (Carters 1999 and 2006). As illustrated in Figure 3, apparel industry offshoring was negligible through 1980 (less than $1 million) and grew dramatically through 2000. These estimates include only offshoring by apparel manufacturers, however, and do not capture the growth of retailers importing directly from abroad.

The majority of all clothing, or cut and sew apparel, sold in the United States is produced overseas. The apparel manufacturing segments that are somewhat sheltered from this trend are: (1) high-end men's, women's and children's fashion that require short runs and quick response times; (2) clothing for U.S. military; and (3) athletic and band uniforms, clerical vestments, costumes, etc., classified as "all other cut and sew apparel."

In 1998, offshoring by apparel manufacturers was almost evenly split between offshoring of apparel production (own offshoring) at 5% of output, and offshoring of other-industry products (extra-industry offshoring) at 5.7% of industry output. Other manufacturing industries' offshoring of apparel products was minimal, at 1.5% of total apparel manufacturing output. During the 1998-03 period, offshoring declined, primarily driven by a fall in own-industry offshoring. This decline is counterintuitive, but likely to be due to the large fall in industry output over this period—shipments fell by 36%. Simply put, firms that are closing down or drastically scaling back operations are not likely to engage in offshoring.

Among small apparel manufacturers contacted for this case study, all have dramatically increased their reliance on offshoring. Two of the three companies were at one point in time traditional manufacturers producing at company-owned factories in the United States. Today, all source between 89% and 100% of their products from third-party contractors based mostly in Asia. For one of the companies, the overseas contract manufacturer also manages the logistics process, delivering final goods to the ultimate retail client. (This type of offshoring is not likely captured in the data set used in the empirical section of this study. If these imports are of final products direct to retailers, they are not considered "parts" in Schott's data, and neither would they be registered as inputs for manufacturers.)

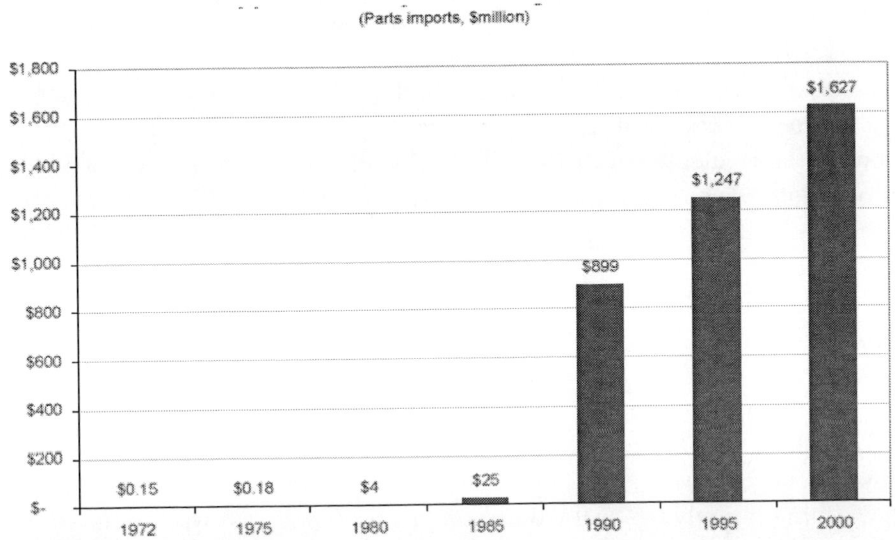

Parts imports for SIC 23. Source: Schott 2004.

Figure 3. Apparel Industry Offshoring Estimates.

U.S. apparel manufacturers have largely kept design, management, and the coordination of the logistics process in the United States. This is the competitive advantage of both small and large U.S. apparel manufacturers: in-house design, marketing, and sales in conjunction with manufacturing expertise and offshored manufacturing. While large mass retailers (e.g., Wal-Mart, Kohl's, etc.) may be able to also offshore the design of basic fashion in addition to production, it is less likely that specialty retailers (e.g., the Gap, Ann Taylor, etc.) or higher end department stores (e.g., Nordstrom, Bloomingdales, etc.) will choose overseas designers or would be able to find effective overseas designers. Specialty retailers view designs and branding as their intellectual property (IP). Higher end department stores might be willing to buy from foreign designers, but may not be able to find designers with implicit knowledge of the U.S. market. In the buyer-driven apparel industry, it will be the decisions of the large retailers, including the decision to offshore design, that may determine the course of the apparel manufacturing industry in the United States. However, the need for close proximity to the catwalks and to consumers has maintained some space for American apparel manufacturers, albeit in a much reduced form compared to 30 years ago. This concentration on sales is confirmed by a look at changes in the occupational distribution of apparel employment. Employment in production occupations decreased by 30% between 1989 and 1997 while employment in sales occupations decreased by only 14%. The perception that design is staying in the U.S. is less clear as employment in research and design occupations decreased by 27%. (See discussion of data in the previous section for a description of data sources and calculations.) In part, this could reflect a mixed picture of production related engineering jobs being eliminated while clothing design jobs remained strong.

Insourcing in Industry

Unlike many manufacturing industries, there has been little foreign investment in the apparel sector. From 1990-1997, the stock of foreign direct investment (FDI) in the apparel industry increased by $389 million, accounting for only 0.5% of industry shipments (compared with an increase of 4.3% of shipments for manufacturing overall). Between 1998 and 2003, FDI again grew by only 0.6% of shipments compared to a 3.0% increase in manufacturing overall. General industry sources and firm interviews all confirm the generally very small levels of insourcing in the apparel industry.

SMEs in Industry

Because of the apparel industry's limited economies of scale, higher labor-intensity, and fragmented retail market, apparel manufacturing has historically been dominated by small manufacturers. More recently, this situation has become more acute with small- and medium-size enterprises (SMEs) accounting for close to three-quarters (72.6%) of total apparel industry employment in 2003 and very small firms accounting for 15.7% of total industry employment.[19] However, it is also important to point out that firms of all sizes are shedding employment rather than gaining, so that the relative resilience of smaller manufacturers could be due to larger firms shrinking into smaller firms.

Firm Level

Latest available data for the period 1998-2003 show the strong growth of SMEs as a share of total apparel manufacturing employment. As total apparel manufacturing sector employment has declined from 671,241 in 1998 to 303,654 in 2003, there have been job losses in apparel manufacturing firms of all sizes. However, job losses among large firms have been greater than among SMEs. For example, large apparel manufacturing firms' share of total employment fell by 13.8% during this five-year period compared to a relative decline of 1.8% for large manufacturing firms overall. At the same time, small apparel manufacturing firms increased their share by 13.8%. The share of employment accounted for by very small apparel manufacturers grew by 6.4% compared to 1.0% for all very small manufacturers.

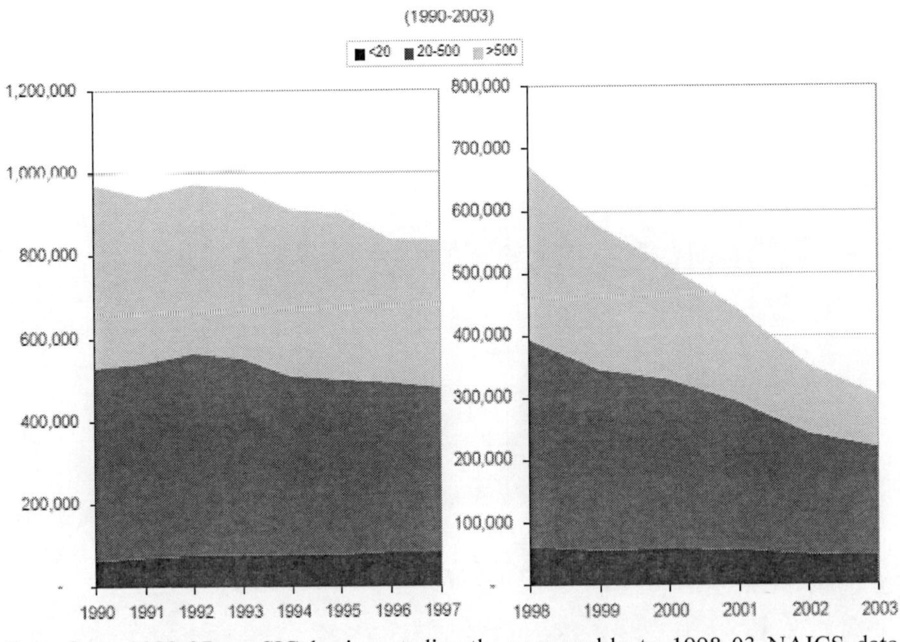

Data from 1990-97 on SIC basis not directly comparable to 1998-03 NAICS data. Source: Small Business Administratio.

Figure 4. Employment in Apparel Industry by Firm Size.

Establishment Level

Looking at apparel manufacturing establishments, one finds similar and more pronounced trends in the share of SMEs in overall apparel manufacturing establishments and employment. SMEs represented 99.0% of all apparel manufacturing establishments in 1975, increasing to 99.7% in 2004. Similarly, SME establishments accounted for 87.2% of total manufacturing sector employment in 1975 and 89.3% in 2003. At the aggregate level, SMEs have been increasing their share of employment and number of establishments over the past 30 years, in a long SME-dominated sector. A more detailed analysis points to rapid growth in the number and overall share of employment of very small apparel manufacturing establishments (those with less than 20 employees) and an increasing loss of very large establishments (those with more than 500 employees). (See Tables 3 and 4.)

Table 3. Apparel Manufacturing Establishments (NAICS 315): Percentage of Employment by Size Category, 1975-2003

Year	Less than 20	Less than 500	More than 500
1975	6.8	87.2	12.9
1980	6.6	85.4	14.6
1985	7.1	83.5	16.5
1990	8.1	84.5	15.4
1995	9.6	81.6	18.4
2000	11.9	82.4	17.3
2002	14.7	86.2	13.8
2003	16.1	89.3	10.7

Source: U.S. Bureau of the Census, *County Business Patterns*.

Table 4. Apparel Manufacturing Establishments (NAICS 315): Percentage of Establishment in Each Size Category, 1975-2004

Year	Less than 20	Less than 500	More than 500
1975	52.5	99.0	0.8
1980	50.5	99.0	1.1
1985	57.5	99.0	1.0
1990	61.8	99.2	0.8
1995	67.2	99.0	0.9
2000	70.3	99.3	0.7
2003	76.3	99.8	0.3
2004	76.3	99.7	0.4

Source: U.S. Bureau of the Census, County Business Patterns.

Case 2: Auto Parts

The auto parts industry illustrates how outsourcing affects industries in very complex ways. On the one hand, the industry has been the beneficiary of the growth in outsourcing (domestic and offshore) by major motor vehicle manufacturers. This has devolved more business to U.S. parts and component suppliers. However, this has occurred in tandem with increasing price pressures that have caused many U.S. auto parts manufacturers to either lose markets or move large portions of more standard component manufacturing overseas. Some small auto parts manufacturers have succeeded in this environment by continuously developing new products and even by outsourcing some or all of their production overseas. Those companies that continue to produce domestically in standardized, relatively unsophisticated market segments appear to be losing out to foreign suppliers or the offshore outsourced operations of their domestic competitors.

Case 1 Firm Summary: Apparel Industry

Table 5. Apparel Industry Firm Summary

	Firm A	Firm B	Firm C
Description	**Designs, arranges for manufacture, and markets women's career and sports apparel.**	**Designs, sources, and markets men's and women's apparel.**	**Designs, manufactures, distributes, and markets women's and children's clothes and accessories.**
	286 (54 of these in East Asian branch offices) (1.4% growth over 2004)	370 (39.1% growth over 2004)	172 (9.5% decline from 2004)
	$143.5 million (-8.8%)	$324.0 million (7.3%)	$126.5 million (1.2%)
	• Company founded in 1975 and offshoring since 1977. • In 2005, 89% of products offshored; 11% sourced from the U.S. • Purchased 72% of finished goods from 10 largest manufacturers. • Most of fabrics used in end products come from China, Hong Kong, Korea. • Overseas manufacturers not only produce finished garments, but also handle quota allocation and customs clearances administration; have located branch offices of subsidiaries in Hong Kong and Korea. • Competitiveness based on ability to stay ahead in styling, pricing, quality (both fabrics and end product), and product identity	• Predecessor company established in 1956 based on apparel manufacture; all manufacturing plants sold in 2000. • All production is currently outsourced overseas because of lower costs. • More than 70% of products manufactured by contractors in China in 2005 (benefiting from China's WTO accession and fact that current MOU establishing voluntary quotas on Chinese exports does not include Company B's main product category). • Competitive edge based on in-house design capabilities, real-time connectivity to customers, and international sourcing capabilities.	• Company founded in 1968, but no longer owns any manufacturing facilities. • In 2005, 100% of products manufactured by foreign contractors (up from 90% in 2002). • Operates small offices in Hong Kong, Shanghai and Dong Guan to coordinate and track orders, invoice certain shipments and inspect East Asian factories. • Dong Guan office opened at request of a major customer that accounts for 44% of net sales (moved office from Taiwan to Dong Guan, China).

Table 5. (Continued)

	Firm A	Firm B	Firm C
			• Competitiveness based on offshore outsourcing, company size and financial position.
Insourcing	• None identified.	• None identified.	• None identified.
Conclusions	• Shows consolidation of overseas apparel sourcing among small number of firms. • Illustrates significant managerial as well as production capabilities of overseas manufacturers. • 100% sourcing strategy, although still listed under apparel manufacturing NAICS.	• Significance of electronic connectivity and quick response time to customers. • Transformation from domestic manufacturer to outsourcing of this entire step in the value chain (though still listed under apparel manufacturing NAICS).	• Illustrates power of large retailers in production and management decisions. • Shows shifting perception of what "manufacturing" means: description as a manufacturer although this company does not manufacture apparel (still listed under apparel manufacturing NAICS).

Long ago, vehicle manufacturers also made many of the parts for their cars. Today, a growing majority of parts and components are assembled by large "Tier 1" suppliers. Each automaker tends to work with a handful of these very large Tier 1 suppliers, who in turn source components and parts from a much larger number of smaller manufacturers.

Small manufacturers in this industry tend to be suppliers to the large Tier 1 and Tier 2 auto parts firms, and tend to specialize in a few product lines that require high degrees of capital, skill and efficiency. This allows them to spread outlays for research and development and tools and dies (the equipment used to produce the parts) over multiple contracts—potentially for different vehicle manufacturers. In other words, a fuel injector manufacturer may supply fuel injectors for vehicles produced by multiple vehicle manufacturers.

The market for parts suppliers depends on the number and characteristics of the vehicles being produced. That market is characterized by a mature, slow-growth U.S. market and a more vibrant, higher growth international market, particularly in developing or emerging market economies. U.S. production has been stagnant with total production of passenger cars and trucks peaking in 1999 at 13 million vehicles, while global production has grown much more robustly (Standard and Poor's 2004).

Two broad trends in the automotive market affect the parts industry.[21] First has been the trend towards devolution of manufacturing responsibility away from the end vehicle manufacturers to their major Tier 1 suppliers. Taking a page from the computer electronics industry, automakers are adopting assembly processes that use standardized components that can be assembled easily and quickly at the vehicle assembly plant. Tier 1 firms are therefore being asked to take over assembly of larger and larger component systems and to assume more supply chain coordination responsibilities.

Second has been intense price pressure throughout the automotive industry. As vehicle manufacturers compete for market share, they have placed considerable pricing demands on all of their suppliers. Cost and productivity improvements are often written into long-term supply contracts between vehicle manufacturers and their suppliers. A survey of supplier companies by the Center for Automotive Research confirms these broad trends, with firms saying they are being asked to take on broader roles in the supply chain and that Tier 1 suppliers are passing price pressures down to lower level suppliers (Center for Automotive Research 2005).

In part because of these trends, employment in the motor vehicle industry (final assembly of cars and trucks) has been stagnant in the past decades, and has experienced a strong downturn in recent years. Meanwhile, employment in the parts and accessories industry increased by 27% between 1990 and 1997. Though not directly comparable because of changes in industry classifications, this expansion was followed by a fall in employment of 14% between 1998 and 2003, a period including the economic recession of 2000-2001. (See Figure 5.)

An examination of the size-distribution of employment shows that the majority of these gains and losses were among larger firms with over 500 employees. In particular, the fate of giants such as Visteon and Delphi (formerly the internal parts operations of Ford and GM respectively), which together employ around 230,000,[22] dictate much of the movement in these aggregate numbers. Employment among smaller manufacturers with fewer than 500 employees has followed overall industry trends, though less drastically. Between 1998 and 2003, when employment among larger firms fell by 16%, employment in small firms declined by only 6%.

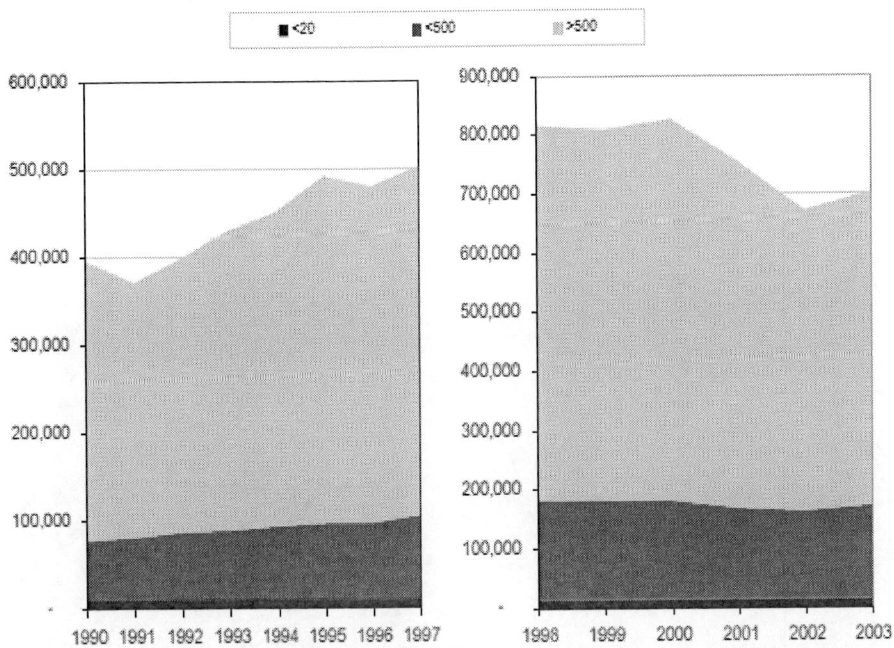

Data from 1990-97 on SIC basis not directly comparable to 1998-03 NAICS data. Source: Small Business Administration.

Figure 5. Employment in the Motor Vehicle Parts & Accessories Industry by Firm Size (1990-2003).

Offshoring in the Industry

To some extent, the auto parts industry depends on outsourcing—motor vehicle manufacturers' outsourcing of parts and component production to parts suppliers. If vehicle producers kept their parts manufacturing in-house, the industry would look much different today. The U.S. industry has been open to motor vehicle imports and to auto parts imports in particular for some time. Estimates of the size of auto parts offshore outsourcing have increased dramatically over the last few decades. (See Figure 6.)

In differentiating offshoring into component pieces, we estimate that other-industry outsourcing dominates. Other industries, particularly the motor vehicle assembly industry offshored about 14% of the parts industry's shipments in 1998, while own intra-industry offshoring was only 2% and extra-industry offshoring was 6.5% of industry shipments. Likewise, over the 1998-03 period, growth in outsourcing was strongest in other industries, moderate for intra-industry outsourcing and actually negative for extra-industry outsourcing. In other words, based on available data, it does not appear that auto parts companies are themselves major outsourcers. However, other manufacturers, most likely Tier 1 suppliers and auto manufacturers themselves are outsourcing increasing volumes of auto parts and components overseas.

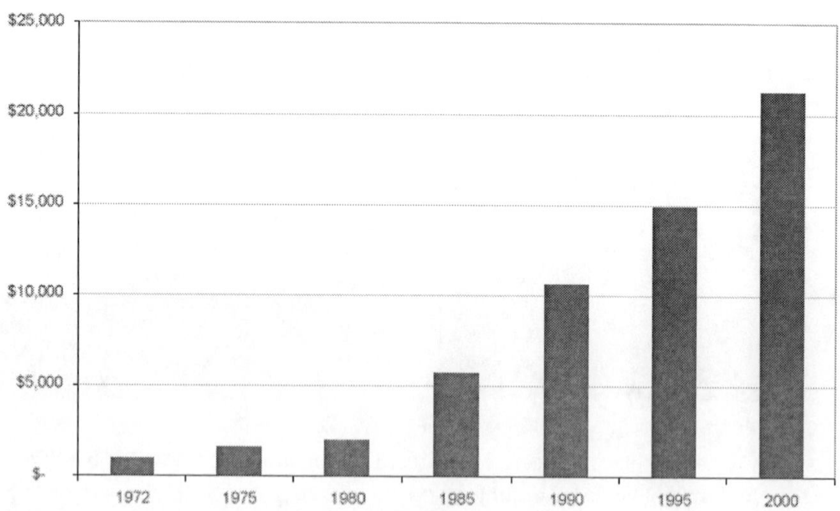

Parts imports for SIC 3714 Source: Schott 2004.

Figure 6. Auto Parts Outsourcing Estimates (Parts imports, Million $).

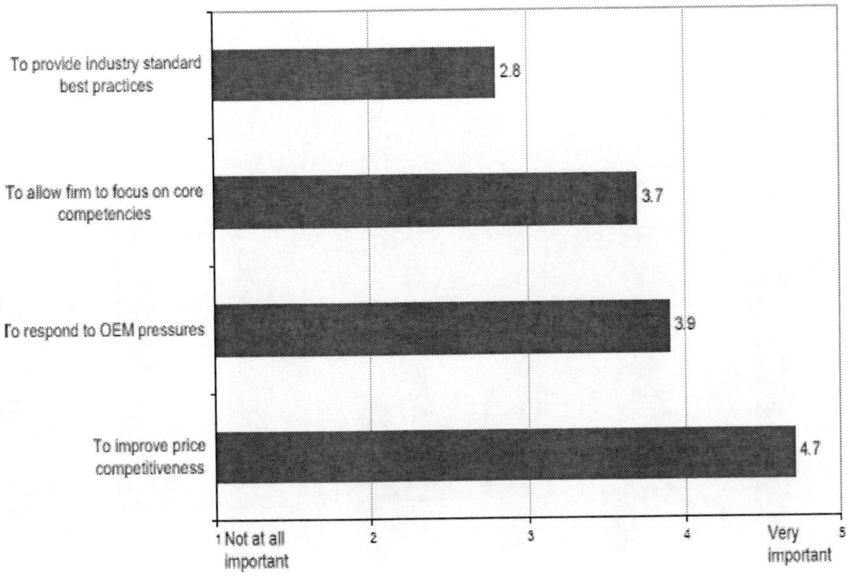

Source: Reproduced from Center for Automotive Research 2005.

Figure 7. Auto Suppliers Reasons for Outsourcing. ("Please rate the following factors in terms of their importance in driving your company to outsource.").

Secondary research confirms these general views. A survey of major supplier companies found that executives "generally frown upon" outsourcing in part because of the time-critical nature of assembly and the emphasis placed on internal capabilities and expertise (Center for Automotive Research, 2005). Nevertheless, a large number of supplier firms do engage in outsourcing of various types, with price concerns being the primary motivator. (See Figure 7.) It is interesting to note that among the activities being outsourced, those most likely to be outsourced to foreign suppliers (offshored) include those activities related to the manufacturing process. Unlike many other industries where the engineering and product design tends to stay nearest to the customer, in auto parts, a full 86% of respondents who outsourced product design did so to overseas firms (Figure 8). This could be a response to the evolution of design and engineering skills among U.S. auto parts manufacturers, where design and engineering is a relatively new offering and is often a response to pressures and requests from Tier 1 suppliers and vehicle manufacturers.

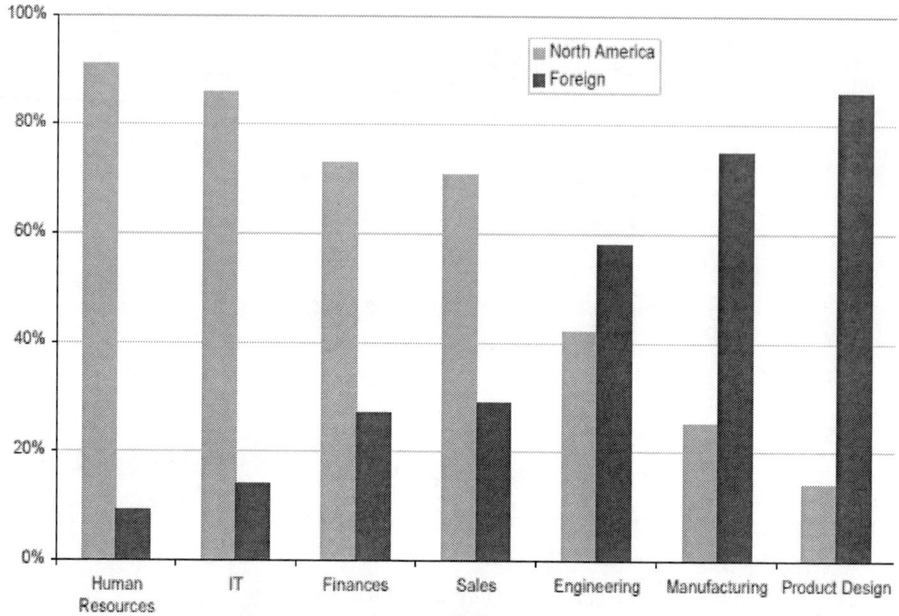

Source: Reproduced from Center for Automotive Research 2005.

Figure 8. Auto Parts Outsourcing Location Decisions. (Of parts suppliers who outsource a given function, where has it been outsourced?).

The small manufacturers examined in this case study had varied experiences with offshoring. All of those contacted through this study report being affected by offshoring in significant ways, some negative and others positive. Nearly the entire range of auto parts products are being offshored, from simple pieces through complex assemblies. The auto industry has a history of international supply chain integration, particularly in the auto parts trade between the United States, Canada and Mexico. One manufacturer, who supplies relatively simple pieces, reported losing significant business due to offshoring of Tier 1 suppliers. The nature of their products is such that they do not change and are generally high-volume runs. Therefore, they are conducive to being manufactured in low-cost locations, shipped, and stored in warehouses near the final assembly plant. In this situation, this small manufacturer's convenient location near vehicle assembly lines is less an asset than it otherwise would be.

At the other end of the spectrum, Company A has entirely offshored its own production. While original product design and development took place in the United States, the company decided to move all production overseas to

Mexico and China. Company A's products are high-value, low-volume, complex components and include proprietary technologies that give it a market edge. But, as a young company (founded only in 1999), the company could not expand internal manufacturing capacity quickly enough to meet market demands. Offshoring has therefore enabled it to grow and serve new clients while improving its products. In particular, offshoring offers the promise of being able to reduce costs and therefore expand its market.

Insourcing in Industry

Insourcing in the auto industry overall has been strong. While domestic production by U.S. firms has been falling, foreign transplants have picked up much of the slack to keep total U.S. production relatively stable. Japanese firms Toyota, Honda and Nissan, for example, have invested heavily in the United States, as have European manufacturers. While well-known, it is worth noting that this foreign insourcing has not been particularly intense when seen from the perspective of manufacturing overall. Between 1998 and 2004, $18.4 billion of FDI flowed into the auto industry, but this amounted to just 3% of sales, the same intensity of FDI as in manufacturing overall. (This amount was divided between motor vehicle manufacturing, which received $7.5 billion and motor vehicle parts manufacturing, which received $6.7 billion.)

Despite this increase in the U.S. operations of foreign auto firms and foreign auto supply firms, indications are that U.S. parts suppliers have had a relatively tough time obtaining supply contracts with them. Previous research has found that foreign auto assemblers have "tight" supplier networks, one reason for the high concentration of foreign-owned suppliers near foreign-owned auto assembly plants (Klier 1998). Those interviewed all expressed the need to develop closer ties with the growing transplant operations, but expressed equal frustration at executing this strategy. Industry sources suggest that foreign vehicle assembly plants tend to prefer to source from the same suppliers that supply them in their home markets. In other words, insourcing at the vehicle assembly level is accompanied by insourcing at the auto parts level as companies bring over their auto parts suppliers to supply their new assembly plants. Among firms interviewed, the exception was company A which has seen a growing portion of sales destined for foreign assembly operations, growing from 20% of sales in 2003 to 37% in 2005.

Case 2 Firm Summary: Automotive Parts Industry

Table 6. Automotive Parts Industry Firm Summary

	Firm A	Firm B	Firm C
Description	Designs, develops, and markets proprietary high-tech systems for Tier1 suppliers and vehicle manufacturers. Young firm has grown dramatically.	Manufacturer of fasteners for vehicle assembly. Firm with rich traditions in auto industry, founded in 1917, auto industry accounts for 85% of sales. Specializes in high-volume lots produced to client specifications. Firm has struggled recently.	Produces engineered trim materials for primarily automotive applications, but also marine and industrial uses. Has been auto supplier from its founding in 1920.
Size & Growth (1yr) Employees	58 (23%)	376 (-11%)	350 (increasing)
Sales	$35.7 million (9%)	$90.7 million (-5%)	$200 million (increasing)
Offshoring	• Company used to produce in-house. • Offshored all production to lower cost countries for cost reasons – lower costs in order to penetrate beyond luxury market. • Third parties manufacture in Mexico and China. • Offshoring of Tier1 suppliers is key source of their business.	• Firm does not outsource - manufactures all products from its Michigan plants. • Competitors and its clients (Tier 1 suppliers) have been offshoring significantly, and this has placed enormous pricing and other pressures on the company.	• Company manufactures all of its products, also has plant in Germany. • Supplies European market through German plant, but for the most part produces domestically.

	Firm A	**Firm B**	**Firm C**
	• Their own offshoring is key to their growth – would not have been able to grow as quickly as they have without it. (though this does little for their U.S. employment)		• Reports pricing pressures from clients, but has been able to introduce new, differentiated products.
Insourcing	• Market for U.S. origin vehicle manufacturers is stagnant. • Major growth in U.S. is from transplant assembly, and also for global market served from contract manufacturers.	• Has had no success at penetrating transplant assembly market.	• Sales are primarily to U.S. automakers (and suppliers), but also Mazda and Nissan. • Domestic manufacturers (and their overseas operations) are their primary clients.
Conclusions	• Shows how offshoring can help small innovative manufacturers leverage capacity to compete.	• Significantly affected by offshoring which has eroded its market. Product line has not evolved and company has had a hard time entering new markets.	• Company has managed to maintain significant U.S. employment because of constant upgrading and introduction of new materials/products

Case 3: Semiconductors

The U.S. semiconductor industry embraced offshoring early on.[23] In the face of severe competition from Japan, U.S. manufacturers of memory devices invested in low-cost offshore assembly facilities in the 1970s. Offshoring has continued in subsequent years to include fabrication, design and testing services. During this time, independent and specialized contract manufacturers emerged in East Asia, changing the global landscape of the industry. The establishment of specialized semiconductor foundries in East Asia enabled the growth of U.S. "fabless" semiconductor companies—those predicated on a model of outsourcing the actual production of semiconductors to third-party fabrication labs, or "fabs." East Asian contract manufacturers have increase-ingly undertaken larger shares of the assembly and fabrication activities, allowing U.S. firms to focus on innovation and product design. However, the trend toward offshoring even these design activities challenges the continued competitiveness of U.S. "fabless" semiconductor companies. Small manufacturers seem to have so far been positively affected by offshoring in the industry, albeit to a different degree, as compared to large manufacturers.

Overview of Industry

Semiconductors, such as microprocessors and memory devices based on integrated circuits (ICs), are the building blocks of an increasing array of electronics and telecommunications industries. Integration of semiconductors with computing and communication technologies has been critical in the high technology revolution of the past decades. While semiconductors have greatly enhanced productivity and made the design and use of other technology-based products easier, production of semiconductors involves one of the most complex and advanced manufacturing processes. The global semiconductor industry was estimated to be approximately $227 billion in 2005, of which memory devices amounted to $48.7 billion. (World Semiconductor Trade Statistics, 2005).

The global semiconductor industry has expanded substantially in the last three decades due to declining costs and the industry's integration with the rapidly growing consumer electronics and communications equipment industries. However, performance of this industry in the United States during the same period has been affected by a number of factors, including global competition, domestic recessions, and increasing attention to innovation and product development. The U.S. semiconductor industry established its early lead in memory devices (DRAM) in the 1970s. However, in the 1980s, Japanese firms steadily gained market share over U.S. firms. By the mid-1980s, competition from Japan forced many U.S. firms to exit the memory market and focus on higher value microprocessor components including processors, micro-controllers, and micro-peripheral devices. American firms' market share in memory products plummeted from 75% in 1980 to less than 20% in 1990 (Macher, Mowery, and Hodges 1999). Maturing Japanese memory device manufacturers and emerging South Korean semiconductors firms compelled the U.S. semiconductor industry to focus on product innovation and development and management of manufacturing process technologies. While the Korean and Taiwanese firms dominated the memory segment of the semiconductor market in the 1990s,[24] the U.S. industry revived itself, riding the increasing demand for design-intensive, digital signal processor components in the early 1990s.

The U.S. semiconductor industry was also challenged by the superior product quality of Japanese firms who were early adopters of techniques such as statistical process control, total quality management and total preventive maintenance. At the same time, the higher productivity

of Japanese and Taiwanese firms further depressed the performance of U.S. firms. Nonetheless, by the mid-1990s, U.S. firms had responded to the quality and productivity challenges from Asian countries and had steered towards higher value-added products where higher production costs were less of a concern.

To fully understand the global competitive landscape in the semiconductor industry, the performance of U.S. firms, emergence of specialized contract manufacturers and the impact of offshoring on the competitiveness of the U.S. semiconductor industry, one needs to first understand the various segments of the semiconductor industry value chain. The semiconductor value chain comprises four major sets of activities: design and prototyping, fabrication, assembly, and testing. (See Figure 9.) Each of these four segments has unique structural characteristics, varied levels of contribution from small, medium and large firms, and different degrees of offshoring.

Except for a handful of companies like IBM and Intel (known as integrated design manufacturers) that are engaged in all parts of the industry's value chain, companies in the United States and elsewhere specialize in a specific segment of the chain. Large U.S. companies with strong capital bases have invested in fabrication facilities. In the Asian countries, government-backed, large-scale facilities have emerged to be strong competitors to American facilities in recent decades.

Given the high capital requirements of fabrication facilities,[25] small manufacturers in the semiconductor industry tend to concentrate in the design, assembly, and testing segments of the value chain.

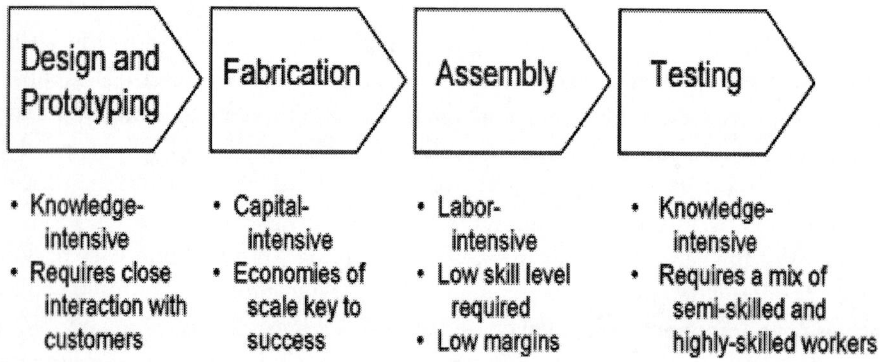

Figure 9. Primary Activities in the Semiconductor Value Chain.

The combined effect of growing global demand for semiconductor-based electronics products and the deepening global competition in all parts of the industry's value chain has kept U.S. employment in semiconductors flat over the last 15 years. For the most part, between 1990 and 2003, overall employment in the industry has fluctuated in a range between 160,000 and 200,000 workers. However, the effects of the "dot.com" boom of the late 1990s and the subsequent economic recession are visible in the employment figures which are marked by a sharp increase around 2000-2001 to a high of over 225,000, followed by a sharp decline in 2003 to a 15-year low of 146,700.

A closer look at the distribution of employment by firm size suggests that a major component of the fluctuation in overall industry employment between 1990 and 2003 has been caused by change in employment among large firms with more than 500 employees. Large firms dominate the semiconductor industry, accounting for almost 85% of industry employment (Figure 10). This share of large firms in total industry employment has remained unchanged during the period of analysis 1990-2003. Employment in very small semiconductor firms (less than 20 employees) has increased moderately from 2,189 in 1990 to 3,020 in 2003, a moderate growth of 38% over 14 years. The employment base of small companies with less than 500 employees shrank by 15% during the same period.

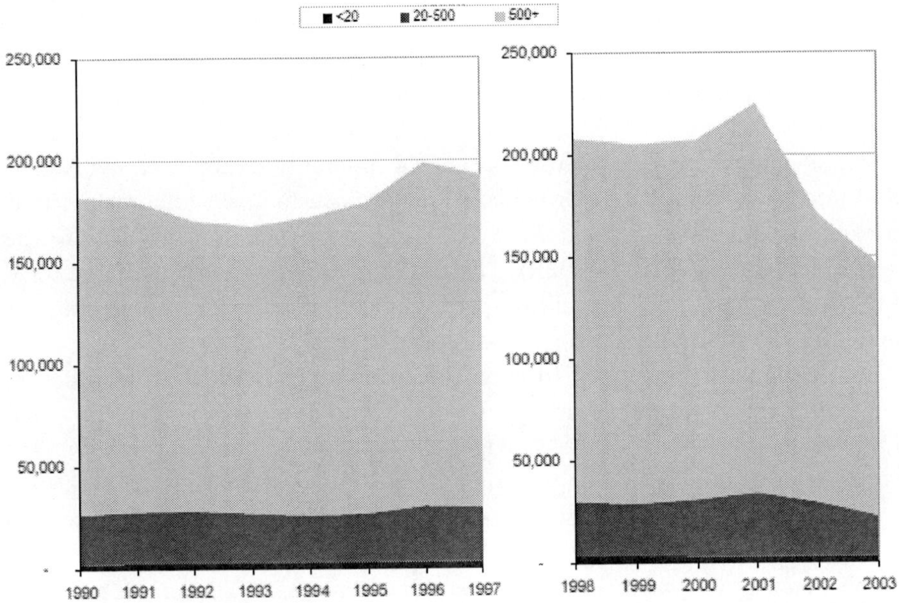

Data from 1990-97 on SIC basis not directly comparable to 1998-03 NAICS data.
Source: SBA Office of Advocacy.

Figure 10. Employment in Semiconductor Industries by Firm Size.

Offshoring in the Industry

Offshoring has been a cornerstone of the U.S. semiconductor industry for decades. The earliest offshore investment in semiconductors was made by Fairchild Semiconductor in Hong Kong in 1961. Over the subsequent four decades, U.S. firms have invested heavily in low-cost regions, particularly in Asia and Latin America, to extend their production base and take advantage of competitive labor costs.

Assembly was the first segment of the industry's value chain to be offshored. Functional separation from other closely connected activities, ease of execution, products' higher value-to-weight ratio and availability of low-skilled workers at very low costs catalyzed offshoring of assembly-related activities. The result of this phase of offshoring was the increased cost competitiveness of the American semiconductor companies and dramatic falls in end-product prices generating enormous consumer surpluses despite job losses among companies in the United States. Although Mexico and El Salvador received assembly investments in the 1970s, East Asia soon emerged as the preferred offshoring destination. U.S. companies employed nearly 100,000 workers in offshore assembly plants by 1977, compared to 114,000 domestic employees, of whom 64,000 were directly involved in production (Brown and Linden 2005). In parallel to the establishment of offshore assembly plants by U.S. firms, specialized assembly contractors evolved in developing economies that provided a range of customized integrated circuit packaging. In 1978, around 80% of U.S. semiconductor production was assembled abroad (Flamm 1985). The figure is now estimated at above 95%, with most remaining U.S. facilities predominantly engaged in prototyping and defense related activities (Brown and Linden 2005).

In contrast to assembly, offshore investments in fabrication facilities by U.S. companies have occurred less frequently and in the more recent past. The irrelevance of labor cost advantages in a capital-intensive activity, and concerns over quality and engineering talent limited offshoring of fabrication by U.S. firms. Instead, offshore fabrication of U.S.-designed chips occurs mainly on an outsourced basis to "foundries"[26] that were established and are being managed by government-backed programs in Taiwan, China and Singapore.[27] Large integrated device manufacturers, like IBM, also offer foundry services, but the pure-play companies are the most important source of fabrication services.

Table 7. Top Five "Pure-Play" Foundries, 2004

Company	**Country**	**2004 Revenues ($ million)**	**2004 Share of Total (%)**
Taiwan Semiconductor Manufacturing Corporation (TSMC)	Taiwan	$7,648	46%
United Microelectronics (UMC)	Taiwan	$3,900	23%
Chartered Semiconductor	Singapore	$1,103	7%
Semiconductor Manufacturing International Corporation (SMIC)	China	$975	6%
Vanguard	Taiwan	$474	3%

Source: Brown and Linden (2005).

Although fabrication activities have been moved offshore or outsourced to pure-play foundries, the employment impact of such moves on the U.S. economy, and especially on small manufacturers, is believed to be marginal for two reasons. First, fabrication facilities are highly automated. They require considerably less labor inputs from technicians and operators than assembly operations. Second, although there has been a loss of high-end engineering jobs at fabrication facilities, the rise of the fabless sector has compensated for the loss of high-end engineering jobs. Brown and Linden (2005) mention that according to the Semiconductor Industry Association, U.S. chip firms were estimated to have 103,000 engineers on their payroll, 30% of whom were located offshore. The authors also estimate that offshoring of fabrication may have displaced about 11,000 jobs, including 2,600 engineering jobs. On the other hand, as a direct impact of the offshoring of fabrication to foundries, the U.S. has had a surge of fabless companies that categorize themselves as semiconductor companies but do not produce a single chip themselves. Whereas most of the fabrication facilities have been owned by large companies, most fabless companies have been small and medium enterprises.

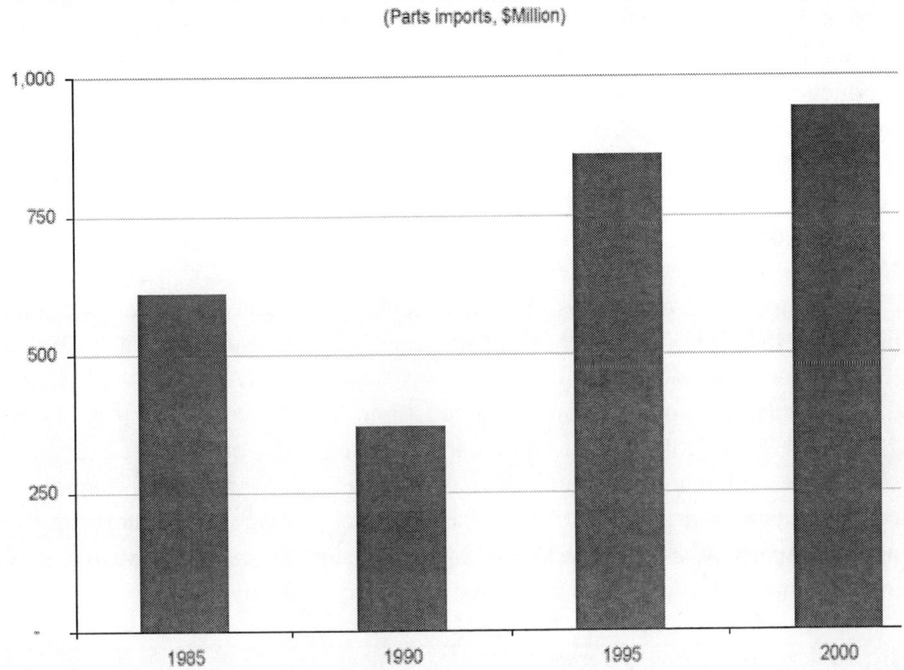

Parts imports for SIC 3674. Source: Schott 2004.

Figure 11. Semiconductor Industry Offshoring Estimates.

More recently, the industry has expanded offshoring of the design segment of the value chain. Although initially the relocation decisions for design jobs were guided by access to markets and proximity to customers, cost savings and access to highly educated scientific talent have been the motivating factors in recent years. IBM and LSI Logic established design centers in Japan and Western Europe in the 1970s. Design-related investments were made in East Asia in the 1980s to customize designs to local market needs. However, in the 1990s and in recent years, design services have been offshored to India and China purely for cost reduction reasons.

Semiconductor Industry Offshoring Estimates

Small semiconductor firms in the United States appear to have taken full advantage of offshoring to stay competitive in the market. All three small companies studied as part of this case have offshored most of their fabrication, assembly, testing and shipping functions to East Asia, keeping a major share of design, R&D, marketing, contracting and management functions in house. These companies state three prime reasons for offshoring. First, outsourcing production activities reduces the burden of large-scale investments in fabrication facilities. Second, working with independent contractors allows them flexibility in manufacturing as they try to respond to the varying demands of a wide range of customers with innovative, customized designs. Third, with the East Asia region becoming the most critical source of revenues for these small U.S. firms, servicing customers directly from the same region reduces supply chain complexities and keeps costs low. These companies have taken equity positions in the foundries they subcontract with, possibly to keep certain management control over their operations and product delivery. All of the three companies studied have expanded their workforce between 2004 and 2005 and have sold to international producers of consumer electronics, computers and communication devices. While the overall performance of these companies has been a better-than-industry average, it is interesting to note company C's announcement of its desire to exit the business of manufacture and sale of semiconductor devices completely.

Insourcing in Industry

Unlike the auto parts industry, insourcing in the semiconductor industry has been less intense in the last few decades, with foreign direct investment increasing by $1.8 billion between 1998 and 2003. Despite the innovation leadership exhibited by the U.S. companies, the stock of FDI was $13.7 billion in 2003 in this knowledge-intensive sector, much of it in strategic, advanced fabrication-related areas where foreign firms aspire to establish their foothold in the U.S. market. For example, Philips of the Netherlands, bought VLSI Technology, a major application-specific integrated circuits company with over 2,000 employees in 1999 for nearly $1 billion. One-third of VLSI's employees were fabrication workers (Semiconductor Business News, 1999).

Insourcing has increased in one particular segment of the industry value chain in recent years: design. Brown and Linden (2005) report that many foreign companies maintain a Silicon Valley or other U.S. design center to take advantage of high skills and to have access to U.S. knowledge networks. Hitachi Semiconductor has a semiconductor design group several hundred strong, and Toshiba has a network of seven ASIC design centers around the United States.

SUMMARY FINDINGS FROM CASE STUDIES

Looking across these three case studies, a number of important issues emerge related to offshoring and the performance of small manufacturers. These are explored below according to each of the study's original hypotheses.

Hypothesis 1: Intra Industry Offshoring

Contrary to our hypothesis, offshoring is a business strategy that seems to be employed by both small and large manufacturers. While it is difficult to draw conclusions from only 9 firms, nearly all of these companies offshore production to a greater or lesser extent. In fact, some of these small manufacturers were found to offshore their entire production process, deciding, instead, to concentrate on client relations, product design and marketing. For these companies, offshoring has been an attractive strategy which they see as central to their survival and prosperity. Among the two companies examined that were struggling the most, one had pursued an aggressive offshoring approach and one had limited offshoring activity. Also contrary to our hypothesis, offshoring seems to directly affect the market segments where small firms are active. Small apparel and auto parts companies operate in market niches where offshoring pressures are acute.

Why do small manufacturers outsource? Cost reduction appears to be a consistent motivation, though other strategic elements vary among industries. For example, in the semiconductor industry, firms indicate a number of newly established companies predicated on a "fabless" offshoring model.

Case 3 Firm Summary: Semiconductor Industry

Table 8. Semiconductor Industry Firm Summary

	Firm A	Firm B	Firm C
Description	Designs, manufactures, and markets power management semiconductors for mobile electronic devices.	Designs, manufactures, and markets integrated circuits (SRAM, DRAM, and flash memory).	Designs, manufactures and markets memory products (SRAM) and provides connectivity and networking solutions.
Size & Growth (1yr) Employees	200 (9.3%)	386 (24.5%)	281 (7.7%)
Sales	$66.3 million (33.1%)	$181.4 million (0.2%)	$23.6 million (-11.6%)
Offshoring	• Established in 1997. • 100% of manufacturing, assembly, testing, packaging, warehousing and shipping outsourced to independent contractors in Asia. • Competitive advantage on product side is ability to develop proprietary products which meet power application needs of multiple customers. • Competitive advantage on cost side is use of fully depreciated offshore DRAM fabs using advanced analog CMOS process technologies—able to achieve lower costs than other fab-less producers.	(0.2%) • Only 59 of 386 full-time employees located in the United States focusing on subcontractor management, sales and marketing. • R&D is conducted at facilities in the United States, Taiwan, and China • 220 employees are located in Taiwan.	• Established in 1985. • 100% offshored to independent foundries. • Die assembly and testing also offshored. • Outsourced to avoid significant capital investments plus lower labor costs. • R&D accounts for 212 of total 281 full-time employees. 182 of these R&D employees are located in company's India office. 30 are located in U.S. office.

	Firm A	Firm B	Firm C
	• Network of offices with team in Hong Kong overseeing manufacturing	• Company sees its competitive advantage as its active participation in the development and refinement of the manufacturing process technologies. • The company has taken equity position in its foundries in order to have this level of participation in process technology.	• Uses equity arrangements in overseas contractor foundries to secure adequate supply of wafers, especially those involving advanced technologies.
Insourcing	• No discernible insourcing	• No discernible insourcing	• No discernible insourcing.
Conclusions	• Shows how offshoring can help small innovative manufacturers stay close to foreign customers. • Bulk of employees and employee growth is overseas.	• Fabless model based on offshore manufacturing. • R&D overseas with manufacturing; illustrates significance of process innovation. • Equity position taken in overseas fab as a means of securing process technology IP and wafer production capacity.	• In 2006, asset sales and announcement that the company will exit the semiconductor industry.

In addition to saving these companies the manufacturing personnel, capital expenditures, fixed assets, and fixed costs, it places them in close proximity to core customers who are typically East Asian manufacturers of consumer electronics products. In comparison, auto parts suppliers and apparel manufacturers rarely cite proximity to clients as a reason for offshoring.

Hypothesis 2: If upstream and downstream manufacturing activities (e.g., design, R&D, etc.) move overseas, this will have an adverse effect on U.S. small manufacturers.

Our case studies are inconclusive with respect to the offshoring of upstream and downstream activities. In the case of semiconductors, all of the small semiconductor companies examined had significant R&D facilities located abroad as well as in the United States, but we were unable to ascertain whether this outsourcing of R&D activities was followed by a decline in U.S. activity in general. Clearly, though, the movement of final electronic device assembly operations overseas has contributed to the attractiveness of off-shoring among semiconductor companies. In the case of apparel, design, marketing, sales, and distribution remain the purview of small, domestic apparel manufacturers who have largely outsourced only the pure manu-facturing. In other words, manufacturing has been eroded even though design activities have remained in the country—at least for small manu-facturers. Meanwhile, apparel retailers' interest in contracting with offshore, third-party manufacturers has threatened the very business model of apparel manufacturing in the United States. For auto parts suppliers, who are being asked to take on more design activities overall, upstream offshoring has been too new to evaluate.

Hypothesis 3: Insourcing

There has been varied experience with insourcing across the three industry case studies. Apparel and semiconductors have seen limited inflows of foreign investment while offshoring has caused significant production capacity to shift overseas. In the auto parts industry, there has been significant insourcing, but it appears not to be benefiting existing auto parts suppliers, who have had a tough time penetrating the markets of foreign vehicle producers. Instead, insourcing in the auto industry has been followed by insourcing in the auto parts industry such that the gains from insourcing have not gone to U.S. firms (though of course, they have employed American workers).

Data Issues

The case studies underscore data concerns. Many of the case study example firms have outsourced all manufacturing operations. These companies continue to see themselves as manufacturers and their revenue streams continue to be based upon manufactured products sold (not on selling R&D or design services). Yet none (or a very small number) of their employees is involved in the direct production of goods. Therefore, while these companies are classified as manufacturers, the process of offshoring has challenged what that means. At broader industry levels, company movement from "manufacturing" to other-industry classifications can significantly alter data. For example, the National Science Foundation (NSF) found that a growing discrepancy between its estimates of U.S. pharmaceutical industry expenditures on R&D and the Pharmaceutical Research and Manufacturers of America (PhRMA)'s estimates of industry R&D were largely explained by a migration of pharmaceutical companies from the manufacturing to wholesale trade NAICS (3254 to 4222) (Ozawa and Franco, forthcoming). We are not sure how much these movements may affect our data on the performance of small manufacturers.

Also interesting to note is how offshoring takes place in some industries. In the semiconductor industry, for example, offshoring of fabrication often includes the warehousing and shipment of semiconductor products by regionally located third-party contractors, since the clients are often overseas as well. A similar process appears to take place occasionally with auto parts and apparel manufacturing, though in these industries the end customer is most often in the United States. This brings up the critical data issue of whether this type of full package offshoring is captured using existing data. We believe it is not, which can distort estimates of offshoring.

VI. CONCLUSION

This study sought to shed light on the impact of offshoring on the future of small manufacturers in the United States. Looking across the two analyses, two broad themes emerge. First, it is clear that offshoring should best be seen as a strategic, business response to increasing global competition rather than as an independent phenomenon. While it is difficult to draw generalizable conclusions from three industry case studies, the cases combined with research from secondary sources illustrate that small firms have used offshoring strategies either reactively or proactively to remain globally competitive. Even in industry segments, such as auto parts, which have a general preference for domestic manufacturing, U.S. firms have been forced to offshore in order to survive. At the empirical level, our results are suggestive that an industry's offshoring has positive benefits in the near term. In addition, offshoring played a strong role in the business models of the more successful companies examined.

On the other hand, manufacturing customers' decisions to purchase from overseas have a clear negative impact on U.S. small manufacturers. For example, large retailers' decisions to bypass domestic apparel manufacturers and purchase from producers in East Asia have had negative implications for both large and small apparel manufacturers in the United States. This suggests that small manufacturers are principally affected by their inability to compete internationally (primarily because of cost concerns), not by offshoring per se.

While the evidence from our research points to a largely positive, though nuanced, picture of the short-term impact of offshoring on U.S. small manufacturers, we have serious concerns about long-term implications. Considering the sector as a whole, manufacturing competitiveness depends on a number of factors along the value-chain. Innovations which generate large, long-term economic payoffs may emerge from anywhere in this "system," and one of the historic reasons for manufacturing success in the United States has been the existence of complete value-chain systems within the country. This study supports the notion that outsourcing can have short-term benefits for firms and even industries. However, we have not been able to properly assess the potential long-term impact of offshoring-induced weakening of the entire system.[28]

The case studies were suggestive that U.S. industries have used offshoring to "move up the value chain" as a response to globalization. However, what will be left as larger and larger portions of value chains are moved overseas, and will that movement diminish the competitiveness of what remains? In semi-conductors, offshoring began with consumer electronics devices assembly and has come to include advanced wafer fabrication and, today, the engineering and R&D centers that are developing the next generations of integrated circuits.

Existing data and estimation techniques are not up to assessing these important long-term issues. As we have shown, existing data capture only broad movements of offshoring and even then in a crude way that may not accurately reflect industry differences in how offshoring is carried out. Better data, perhaps linking long-term, firm-level behavior with more detailed industry import-export data could be applied. Further investigation of employment changes in different manufacturing industry occupations could illuminate the linkages between the offshoring of certain activities and industry performance in the future. Small manufacturers will be struggling with offshoring for some time, and given the underlying importance of these issues to our national competitiveness, it is crucial to understand these processes better.

VII. REFERENCES CITED

Berman, Eli, John Bound, and Zvi Griliches. "Changes in the Demand for Skilled Labor within U.S. Manufacturing: Evidence From the Annual Survey of Manufactures." *The Quarterly Journal of Economics* 109, no. 2 (2003): 367-97.

Bernard, Andrew B., J. Bradford Jensen, and Peter K. Schott. "Importers, Exporters, and Multinationals: A Portrait of Firms in the U.S. That Trade Goods," *NBER Working Paper* no. 11404. Cambridge, MA: National Bureau of Economic Research, 2005.

Bound, John, and G Johnson. "Changes in the Structure of Wages in the 1980s: An Evaluation of Alternative Explanations." *American Economic Review* 82 (1992): 371-92.

Brown, Clair, and Greg Linden. "Offshoring in the Semiconductor Industry: A Historical Perspective." Paper presented at the *2005 Brookings Trade Forum on Offshoring of White-Collar Work.* Washington, DC: The Brookings Institution, 2005.

Bureau of the Census. "County Business Patterns." Washington, DC: U.S. Department of Commerce, Bureau of the Census, various years.

Bureau of Economic Analysis. "Foreign Direct Investment in the United States." Washington, DC: U.S. Department of Commerce, Bureau of Economic Analysis, 2006a.

Bureau of Economic Analysis. *Industry Economic Accounts: Gross Domestic Product by Industry Data,* April 27, 2006. Washington, DC: U.S. Department of Commerce, Bureau of Economic Analysis, 2006b. Available from http://www.bea.gov/bea/dn2/gdpbyind_data.htm [cited May 10, 2006].

Bureau of Labor Statistics. *Current Employment Statistics.* Washington, DC: U.S. Department of Labor, Bureau of Labor Statistics. Available from http://www.bls.gov/ces#data [cited 2006].

Carters, Inc. "Form 10-K." April 1, 1999. Carters, Inc. "Form 10-K." March 15, 2006.

Center for Automotive Research. "Changing Business Dynamics in the Automotive Supplier Sector." Ann Arbor, MI: Center for Automotive Research, 2005.

Chapple, K., A. Markusen, G. Schrock, D. Yamamoto, and P. Yu. "Gauging Metropolitan 'High-Tech' and 'I-Tech" Activity.'" *Economic Development Quarterly* 18, no. 1 (2004): 10-29.

CHI Research, Inc. *Small Serial Innovators: The Small Firm Contribution to Technical Change,* U.S. Small Business Administration, Office of Advocacy, 2003.

CNN Money, 2005. "Motorola Outsources $30 Billion." Available from http://money.cnn.com/2000/05/31/companies/motorola/.

Council of Economic Advisers. *Economic Report of the President 2001.* Washington, DC: Government Printing Office, 2001.

Council on Competitiveness. *Innovate America: National Innovation Initiative Summit and Report.* Washington, DC: Council on Competitiveness, 2005.

DeVaul, Diane. *Advancing U.S. Manufacturing: Challenges Facing Small Manufacturers.* Washington, DC: Northeast Midwest Institute, 2004.

Doeringer, Peter, and Audrey Watson. "Apparel." In *U.S. Industry in 2000: Studies in Competitive Performance*, edited by David C. Mowery. Washington, DC: National Academy Press, 1999.

Feenstra, Robert C. "Integration and Disintegration in the Global Economy." *Journal of Economic Perspectives* 12 (1998): 31-50.

Feenstra, Robert C., and Gordon H. Hanson. "Globalization, Outsourcing, and Wage Inequality." *The American Economic Review* 86, no. 2 (1996).

______"The Impact of Offshoring and High Technology Capital on Wages: Estimates for the United States, 1979-1990." *Quarterly Journal of Economics* 114, no. 3 (1999): 907-40.

Flamm, Kenneth S. "Internationalization in the Semiconductor Industry," in *The Global Factory: Foreign Assembly in International Trade*, edited by Joseph Grunwald and Kenneth S. Flamm, 38-136. Washington, DC: The Brookings Institution, 1985.

Franco, Quindi, and Sushanta Mohapatra. "Offshoring and Manufacturing Productivity." Washington: DC: SRI International Report for Manufacturing Extension Partnership, 2004.

Franco, Quindi, Farida Lim, John Mathieson, Sushanta Mohapatra, and Jennifer Ozawa. "Behavior and Results of Top U.S. Manufacturing

Firms." Washington, DC: SRI International Report for Manufacturing Extension Partnership, 2004a.

______ "Behavior and Results of Top Foreign Manufacturing Firms." Washington, DC: SRI International Report for Manufacturing Extension Partnership, 2004b.

Harrison, Bennet, and M Kelley. "Outsourcing and the Search for 'flexibility'." *Work, Employment & Society* 7, no. 2 (1993): 213-35.

Heshmati, Almas. "Productivity Growth, Efficiency and Outsourcing in Manufacturing and Service Industries." *Journal of Economic Surveys* 17, no. 1 (2003): 79-112.

Hoover's Company Reports, www.hoovers.com.

Kahn, Jeremy. "Small Firms Find That Outsourcing Cuts Both Ways." *Fortune Small Business* 2004.

Kilcoyne, Patrick. "High-Tech Occupations by Metropolitan Statistical Area." In *Occupational Employment and Wages, 2001*. Washington, DC: U.S. Department of Labor, Bureau of Labor Statistics, 2003.

Klier, Thomas. "Geographic Concentration in U.S. Manufacturing: Evidence from the U.S. Auto Supplier Industry." Chicago, IL: Federal Reserve Bank of Chicago, 1998.

Luria, D. "U.S. Component Manufacturing at a Crossroads: Region-Loyal Production & Global Manufacturing Deflation." Paper presented at the *Conference on Supply Chain Governance and Regional Governance in the Global Economy*, Univeristy of Wisconsin-Madison, 2002.

Macher, Jefferey T, David C. Mowery, and David A. Hodges. "*Semiconductors*." In *U.S. Industry in 2000: Studies in Competitive Performance*, edited by David C. Mowery. Washington, DC: National Academy Press, 1999.

Mittelhauser, Mark. "Employment Trends in Textiles and Apparel, 1973-2005." *Monthly Labor Review* August (1997): 24-35.

Nexus Associates. "How SMEs Understand and Respond to Global Manufacturing Challenges." Washington, DC: NIST Manufacturing Extension Program, 2005.

Office for Textiles and Apparel (OTEXA). *Expanded Textile and Apparel Imports and Exports Database.* Washington, DC: U.S. Department of Commerce International Trade Administration. Available from http://otexa.ita.doc.gov/msrpoint.htm [cited July 2006].

Ozawa, Jennifer K., and Quindi C. Franco. "Funding and Regulation of Research: The Role of Government in Health Innovation." In

Comprehensive Medicinal Chemistry II, edited by Peter Kennewell. London: Elsevier Press, forthcoming.

Peregrine Analytics, LLC. "Innovation and Small Business Performance: Examining the Relationship Between Technological Innovation and the Within-Industry Distributions of Fast Growth Firms." Washington, DC: U.S. Small Business Administration, Office of Advocacy, 2006.

Polly, Laura. "Industry and Trade Summary: Motor Vehicles." Washington, DC: U.S. International Trade Commission, Office of Industries, 2002.

Schott, Peter K. "Across-Product Versus Within-Product Specialization in International Trade." *Quarterly Journal of Economics* 119, no. 2 (2004).

Semiconductor Business News. "Philips to Acquire VLSI Technology for $953 Million," *Semiconductor Business News,* May 3, 1999.

Standard and Poor's, Inc. "Industry Surveys: Autos & Auto Parts." New York, NY: Standard and Poor's, 2004.

The Manufacturing Institute, National Association of Manufacturers, and RSM McGladrey. *The Future Success of Small and Medium Manufacturers: Challenges and Policy Issues.* Washington, DC: National Association of Manufacturers, 2006.

U.S. Department of Commerce. *Manufacturing in America. A Comprehensive Strategy to Address the Challenges of U.S. Manufacturing*. Washington, DC: U.S. Government Printing Office, 2004.

U.S. Small Business Administration (SBA). *Firm Size Data: Statistics of U.S. Businesses and Nonemployer Statistics.* Washington, DC: U.S. Small Business Administration, Office of Advocacy. Available from http://www.sba.org/advo/research/data.html [cited 2006].

United Nations Conference on Trade and Development (UNCTAD). *TNCs and the Removal of Textiles and Clothing Quotas, UNCTAD Current Studies on FDI and Development*. New York and Geneva: United Nations, 2005.

Whitford, J, and J. Zeitlin. *Governing Decentralized Production: Institutions, Public Policy, and the Prospects for Inter-Firm Collaboration in U.S. Manufacturing* , 2003. Available from http://bovine. ssc.wisc.edu /supply chain/pdf/whitford-zeitlin-final.pdf [cited 2006].

World Semiconductor Trade Statistics. "WSTS Semiconductor Market Forecast, Autumn 2005." San Jose, CA: World Semiconductor Trade Statistics, 2005.

APPENDIX A: DATA AND ESTIMATIONS METHODOLOGY

Small Business Performance

Initially, we had proposed to look at two small business performance variables: value-added and employment by small firms. Unfortunately, value-added figures from the Economic Census are only available on an establishment basis and not at the firm-level. In other words, small establishments of very large parent firms are combined with small single-establishment firms in the data set. As this would clearly distort results, we instead use employment figures at the firm level exclusively. Specifically, we look at changes in employment in each industry among firms with less than 500 and less than 20 employees. As small businesses would tend to follow overall industry trends, we also look at overall industry performance and among large firms (greater than 500 employees) for controls. Data were assembled at all levels of aggregation from the most disaggregated 6-digit NAICS and 4-digit SIC through higher-level aggregations of related industries. SIC-based data, however, were manually aggregated to the 3-digit and 2-digit level based on available 4-digit data. The original data are from the U.S. Census Bureau's Statistics of U.S. Business, and provided by SBA's Office of Advocacy.

Offshoring

Unfortunately, data are not collected on international offshoring. However, various proxies and estimation methodologies do exist at the industry level, and we use two here. The first approach uses a technique described by Feenstra and Hanson (1996) to estimate industry purchases of imported manufactured intermediate inputs. This is constructed by combining detailed trade data from the International Trade Commission and input-output tables from the Bureau of Labor Statistics[29] indicating the value of intermediate inputs that each industry purchases from every other industry.

Each industry's outsourcing (Oi) is estimated as the sum of the industry's input purchases from each other industry (j) multiplied by the import penetration in that industry (Ij). (See equations below.)

$$I_j = \frac{imports_j}{production_j + imports_j - \exp orts_j}$$

$$O_i = \sum_j input_j \times I_j$$

We further separate offshoring into three components: intra-industry offshoring (Oii), extra-industry offshoring (Oei) and other-industry offshoring (Ooi). Intra-industry offshoring looks only at an industry's imported intermediate purchases of products it produces (the computer and office equipment industry's purchase of imported computer and office equipment). Extra-industry offshoring refers to an industry's purchase of imported intermediates from *other* industries. An example of extra-industry offshoring is the computer industry's purchase of electrical equipment and plastics. Intra- and extra-industry offshoring sum to total industry offshoring for each industry as in Feenstra and Hanson (1996). While both intra- and extra-industry offshoring focus on the purchases and behavior of an industry (i), other-industry offshoring looks at the estimated offshoring of other industries of the products industry i produces. Returning to the computer industry example, other-industry offshoring for the electrical equipment industry include the computer industry's offshoring of electrical equipment. Extra-industry offshoring and other-industry offshoring are related in that, over all industries total manufacturing offshoring equals the sum of intra-industry offshoring and extra-industry offshoring, and also the sum of intra-industry offshoring and other-industry offshoring. Because detailed input-output tables were not available for all years, this method is used only for the NAICS-based calculations of 1998-2003.

The second source for industry offshoring also proxies offshoring by looking at intermediate manufacturing imports at the industry level, but is constructed through a different process. Schott (2004) developed a set of estimates at the four-digit SIC level (1987 revision) from 1972 to 2001 where intermediate imports are defined as the sum of product-level imports categories that contain variants of the word "part." The difference between these two approaches is that the first uses input-output data to estimate offshoring at the industry level, whereas the second uses details of product import descriptions.

It is important to note that data is only available on national product imports, not imports by industry. In other words, data exists on furniture imports, but not whether these are outsourced imports by the furniture industry or imports by the retail furniture sector. Thus, both of these approaches implicitly assume that each industry's imports are closely related to the import share of products in the overall economy. Furthermore, both approaches take a broad interpretation of offshoring to include both related and unrelated purchasing of inputs. While some analysts make a distinction between offshoring and the purchase of standard inputs from unrelated suppliers, this approach calls both offshoring.

Dollar levels of offshoring vary widely across industries, reflecting both the scale of different industries as well as the intensity of offshoring in each industry. To account for these differences, we look at offshoring intensity, or dollar values of offshoring as a share of industry shipments, as well as the change in offshoring over time.

Insourcing

As a proxy for insourcing, we use changes in the stock of foreign direct investment at the industry level on a historical-cost basis. This set of data, from the Bureau of Economic Analysis's International Economic Accounts "Foreign Direct Investment in the United States" series, covers all manufacturing industries, but at a somewhat aggregated mix of 2 and 3- digit SIC and 3 and 4-digit NAICS level. As reported FDI levels can fluctuate widely from year to year (reflecting major investments or sales), we take a three year average FDI position around the years of interest (e.g., 1996-1998 for FDI in 1997). Again, as scale matters in determining the impact of insourcing on performance, we look at changes in FDI intensity or the change in FDI stocks between the beginning and end years divided by total industry shipments.

Some more detailed industries are further reported in a more aggregate fashion. For example, industrial chemicals and organics (SIC 281 and 286) are reported as one industry. The FDI data for this analysis is distributed at the more detailed level assuming FDI intensity changes are evenly distributed across more detailed levels. For those segments where FDI are aggregates across multiple 2-3 digit segments, intensity is likewise distributed across those components.

For example, the detailed computer storage devices industry (SIC 3572) and computer terminals (3575) industries are assumed to have the same change in intensity of their more aggregate computer and office equipment (SIC 357) industry.

Industry Characteristics

We use an employment by occupation approach to measure industry characteristics of industry orientation towards innovation and technology, production, and sales. This general approach has been used often in past research to measure the technology-orientation of industries and regions, and has recently been used to measure issues such as the production-orientation of industries. (See Chapple et al. 2004 and Peregrine Analytics 2006.) Rather than looking at "output" issues such as patents and other technology measures of innovation, an employment approach looks at how concentrated employment in an industry is in certain technology, or other functional occupations. An industry with a high concentration of scientists is presumed to be more science-focused than one whose employees are mostly machinists.

The Bureau of Labor Statistics conducts an employer survey and tabulates employment data by occupation and by industry in its Occupational Employment Statistics (OES) program.[30] For the SIC years, we use data for 1989 (data is not available for every year, this is closest to the start year) and 1997 at the 3-digit SIC level. This data is distributed at the more detailed 4-digit level for the analysis, assuming that industry characteristics are similar in detailed industries as their more aggregate segments. OES first reported survey results on a NAICS basis in 2002, and this was used for the NAICS dataset.

For each industry, we look at the share of industry employment in three sets of occupations: science and technology, sales and related, and production. These were assembled to include broad categories of jobs rather than narrowly defined specific occupations.[31] The exact occupations included in each set are detailed in Table 9.

Table 9.

	Description	Location, Citation
Employment by Firm Size	Percent change in employment in industry segment in firms with <500 & <20 employees 1990-97, and 1998-03. (employer firms only)	U.S. Small Business Administration, Office of Advocacy, based on data provided by the U.S. Census Bureau, Statistics of U.S. Businesses. http://www.sba.gov/advo/research/data.html
Offshoring	Feenstra & Hanson approach – industry purchases of imported intermediate inputs. Based on BLS inputoutput tables for 1998-03. (NAICS Only)	Imports & Exports – U.S International Trade Commission–dataweb.usitc.gov; U.S. General Imports, General customs value; Total Exports, FAS Value BLS Input Output Tables: Department of Labor, Bureau of Labor Statistics, http://www.bls.gov/emp/empind3.htm
	Schott Approach –Sum of product-level imports by industry where import description contains the word "part." (SIC only)	Schott, Peter K. 2004. "Across-Product versus Within-Product Specialization in International Trade." Quarterly Journal of Economics 119(2). Available on P. Schott's website: http://www.som.yale.edu/faculty/pks4/sub_international.htm
Insourcing	Insourcing intensity over period. Change in foreign direct investment position on a historical-cost basis in the United States between periods divided by first period shipments.	Bureau of Economic Analysis, International Economic Accounts, "Foreign Direct Investment in the United States. http://www.bea.gov/bea/di/di1fdibal.htm
Other Industry Characteristics	Production Intensity - % employment in production occupations Sales Intensity - % employment in sales occupations Science and Engineering Intensity - % employment in creative, science and engineering occupations	Bureau of Labor Statistics, Occupational Employment Statistics. http://www.bls.gov/oes/home.htm

APPENDIX B: INTRA-INDUSTRY, EXTRA-INDUSTRY AND OTHER- INDUSTRY OFFSHORING DATA

Variations Across Industries in Intra-Industry, Extra-Industry and Other-Industry Offshoring

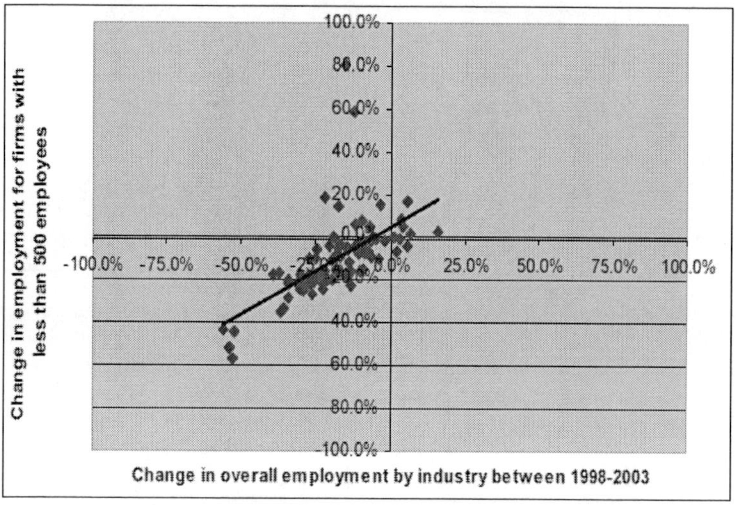

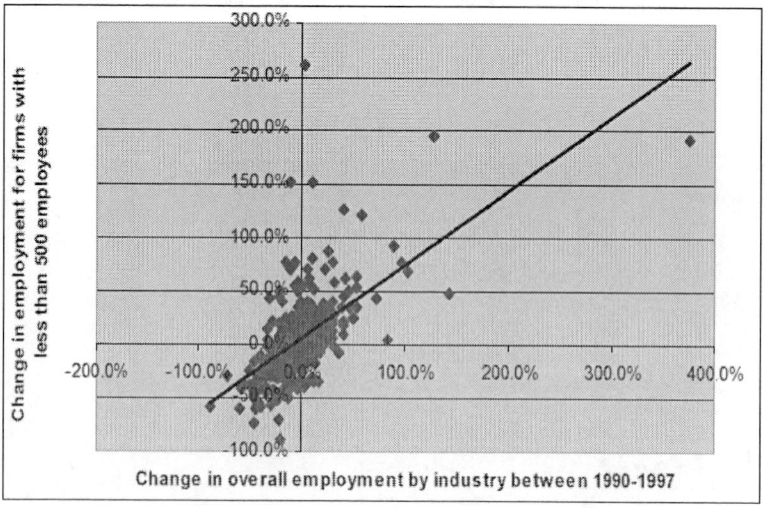

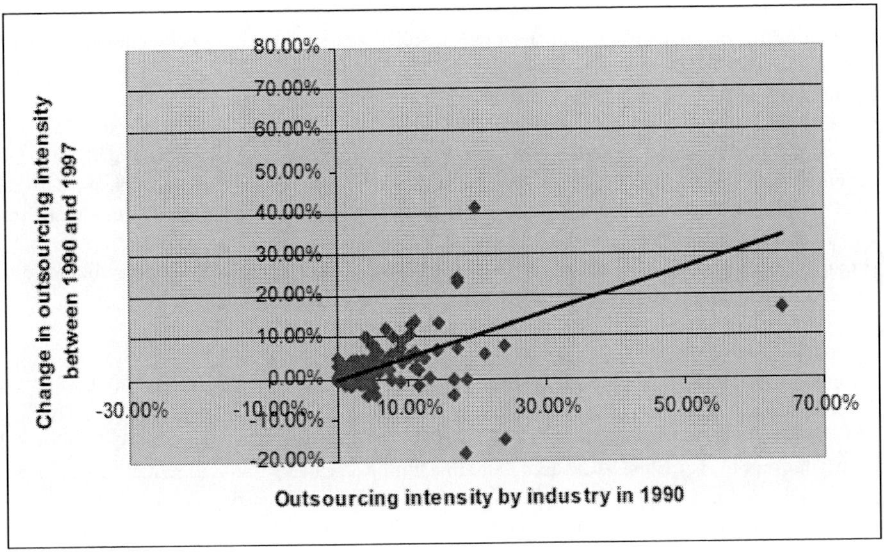

End Notes

[1] For a survey of the productivity literature see Franco and Mohapatra 2004, and Heshmati 2003. On the relationship between outsourcing and labor demand and other issues, see Berman, Bound, and Griliches 2003; Bound and Johnson 1992; Feenstra and Hanson 1996; and Feenstra and Hanson 1999.

[2] Flextronics, for example, was the exclusive design and production firm for the popular Palm Pilot product. See Franco et al 2004a.

[3] See Franco et al. 2004a.

[4] This type of related activity is largely carried out *within* firms and industries so that it is extremely difficult to assess the extent of this type of offshoring (Intel's chip design activities are categorized as "manufacturing" in our economic data).

[5] For example, Honda's U.S. plants build approximately 60% of the 1.35 million Honda vehicles sold in the United States with $13 billion worth of parts purchased from 620 North American suppliers (Franco et al. 2004a).

[6] Not all agencies did this at the same time such that the years around 1997 are often a combination of SIC and/or NAICS data. The Bureau of Labor Statistics' Occupational Employment Statistics survey, for example, only began reporting data on a NAICS basis beginning with 2002. The original NAICS system (1997 NAICS) was modified again, becoming 2002 NAICS. Though there are significant differences in the classification of some industries between the 1997 NAICS and the 2002 NAICS, manufacturing segments were unaffected. Therefore, we freely combine data based on these two NAICS classifications.

[7] The Bureau of Labor Statistics input-output tables are based on the Bureau of Economic Analysis's original 1997 benchmark tables. They were used instead of BEA input-output

tables because BEA's annual tables are only available at the most aggregate level (19 manufacturing industries), and the more detailed benchmark tables corresponding to the 2002 Census were not yet available.

[8] See Chapple et al 2004 and Peregrine 2006.

[9] For example, the near-perfect correlation (0.94, significant at 0.01 level) between change in overall industry employment and change in employment among large firms with over 500 employees, shows that growth or decline in the employment base in any industry between 1998 and 2003 was closely reflected in the growth or decline of employment in larger firms rather than small firms.

[10] Figures for 1987 and 1997 are on a SIC basis, which is not completely comparable to 2003 NAICS basis figures. However, growth trends are consistent throughout.

[11] The general direction of the relationship was negative, although the relationship was not statistically significant.

[12] Although the base models had the same variables relating to insourcing, offshoring and industry characteristics, the NAICSbased models had three variables probing the levels of offshoring in greater detail as compared to just one variable representing the overall offshoring levels for the SIC-based data. In addition, for the SIC-based model, we examined including import intensity and percentage change in import intensity as predictors of change in employment. The inclusion of import data did not alter the sign of relevant variables, so we present our preferred model.

[13] Change in insourcing has a stronger unstandardized coefficient (B = 0.661) and change in offshoring has a stronger negative effect (B = -1.166).

[14] The model explains about 11.6% of all variations across industries in change in employment for very small firms.

[15] Author calculations based on Bureau of Economic Analysis 2006b.

[16] Unless otherwise noted, numbers cited in the apparel case study section refer to calculations by the author described earlier in this report and to SIC 23 prior to 1998 and NAICS 315 from 1998 onwards.

[17] See, for example, Mittelhauser 1997 and UNCTAD 2005.

[18] Author interview with Nate Herman, American Apparel and Footwear Association, June 5, 2006.

[19] Author calculations based on U.S. Small Business Administration 2006.

[20] Unless otherwise noted, the data presented for auto parts refer to the data set assembled in this study and to SIC 3714 for 1997 and prior years and NAICS 3363 after 1997.

[21] Polly 2002 gives a more thorough review of these and other industry trends.

[22] Delphi had 185,200 employees and Visteon had 49,575 in 2005 (Hoover's Company Reports).

[23] Unless otherwise noted, the data presented here refer to the data set assembled in this study and to SIC 3674 for 1997 and prior years and NAICS 334413 after 1997.

[24] By 1997, the Korean firm Samsung had the largest share of the global memory market including SRAM and DRAM products.

[25] Brown and Linden (2005) estimated that fixed investments in a fabrication facility typically amounts to $2 billion to $3 billion for a 300-millimeter wafer fabrication facility.

[26] Foundries are pure-play fabrication facilities that manufacture chips to the specifications of other companies, but do not sell any chip of their own design.

[27] For example, Chartered Semiconductor, a leading foundry based in Singapore, is part-owned by the government. The Taiwanese foundry United Microelectronics (UMC) is government-backed and the largest Chinese foundry Semiconductor Manufacturing International

Corporation (SMIC) has received a major part of its capital from Chinese government agencies.

[28] It is interesting to note that a number of public institutions have emerged over the last decades that, to a certain extent, can serve to offset or counteract this erosion. The Manufacturing Extension Partnership system, for example, is designed to help small manufacturers make linkages and to find the services they need to compete. This can supplant for the erosion of in-house manufacturing expertise and social networks that may be the result of offshoring. It is unclear, though, whether these "artificial" institutions can effectively replace their market predecessors.

[29] The Bureau of Labor Statistics input-output tables are based on the Bureau of Economic Analysis original 1997 benchmark tables. They were used instead of BEA input-output tables because BEA's annual tables are only available at the most aggregate level (19 manufacturing industries), and the more detailed benchmark tables corresponding to the 2002 Census were not yet available.

[30] Recent SBA research instead looked at individual survey responses in the Current Population Survey to construct industry employment concentration data (Peregrine 2006). This was done to circumvent the perceived large-firm bias in the OES system. Their data set, however, reveals a very tight correlation between the two methods.

[31] For a review and comparison of the narrow versus broad approach, see Kilcoyne 2001.

INDEX

2

2001 recession, 2, 3, 6, 16, 17, 19
20th century, 13

9

9/11, 12

A

abatement, 50
access, 75, 77
accounting, 2, 5, 6, 10, 11, 20, 56, 72
acquisitions, 4
adjustment, 13
administrative support, 2, 10, 11, 15, 16, 17, 18
administrators, 16
advancements, 2
age, 15, 17
agencies, 5, 93, 94
aggregation, 87
agriculture, 9
anxiety, 7
apparel industry, 49,50, 52, 53, 54, 56
appropriations, 13
Argentina, 6
Asia, 32, 55, 70, 73, 76, 78, 82
Asian countries, 71
assets, 80
attachment, 14
audit, 10, 11
auto assembly lines, vii, 1, 3
automation, 50
automobile parts, 33
automotive applications, 68

B

Bangladesh, 53
banks, 20
Barbados, 53
barriers, 9
base, 31, 47, 72, 73, 94
BEA, 93, 95
benchmarks, 31
beneficiaries, 4
benefits, 4, 34, 82
beverages, 38
Bhagwati, 8, 21, 22, 23
bias, 95
biotechnology, 7
blue-collar workers, vii, 1, 3, 6, 14
Brazil, 6, 12
building blocks, 70
Bulgaria, 6
Bureau of Labor Statistics, 2, 3, 14, 18, 20, 23, 36, 49, 51, 84, 85, 87, 90, 91, 93, 95
business cycle, 3, 19
business model, 80, 82

business processes, 12
business strategy, 77
businesses, vii, 1, 2, 3, 16, 27, 29, 32, 33, 34, 36, 37, 47, 48, 87
buyer, 51, 54, 56

C

CAD, 52
candidates, 7
capital expenditure, 80
Caribbean, 53
case studies, 26, 27, 29, 33, 34, 47, 49, 77, 80, 81, 82
case study, 28, 30, 54, 66, 81, 94
cation, 76
cell phones, 31
Census, 58, 59, 83, 87, 91, 94, 95
challenges, 29, 70, 71
chemicals, 89
Chicago, 85
children, 54, 60
China, 2, 6, 30, 53, 60, 67, 68, 74, 76, 78
Chinese government, 94
classification, 23, 35, 93
clients, 13, 31, 67, 68, 69, 80, 81
clothing, 49, 50, 54, 56
CNN, 31, 84
coal, 48
coding, 52
combined effect, 41, 42, 46, 72
communication, 70, 76
competition, 5, 13, 70, 71, 72, 82
competitive advantage, 32, 55, 79
competitiveness, 49, 52, 70, 71, 73, 82, 83
competitors, 59, 71
complement, 47
complexity, 26
composition, 2, 4, 13
computer, vii, 1, 2, 3, 6, 8, 9, 10, 11, 16, 18, 20, 36, 39, 48, 52, 62, 88, 90
computer software, 11
computer systems, vii, 1, 2, 3, 6, 18
computer-aided design (CAD), 52
computing, 70
confidentiality, 12, 49
Congress, 1, 2, 4, 13
connectivity, 51, 60, 61, 78
consolidation, 52, 61
construction, 9, 14, 18, 19, 20, 23
consumer surplus, 73
consumers, 4, 56
coordination, 30, 55, 62
correlation, 11, 27, 38, 40, 47, 94, 95
correlation coefficient, 47
correlations, 41
cost, 2, 6, 12, 49, 52, 66, 68, 70, 73, 74, 75, 78, 82, 89, 91
cost saving, 12, 75
Costa Rica, 53
covering, 35
crises, 19
CT scan, 7
cultural differences, 13
customers, 13, 23, 60, 61, 75, 76, 78, 79, 80, 82
cyclical unemployment, 2, 4
Czech Republic, 6

D

data communication, 2, 6
data set, 55, 87, 94, 95
declining industries, 47
Department of Commerce, 53, 83, 86
Department of Labor, 51, 84, 85, 91
dependent variable, 41
designers, vii, 1, 3, 55
detection, 48
developing countries, 4, 6, 49, 52
devolution, 62
differentiated products, 69
direct investment, 3, 4, 29, 32, 34, 35, 37, 41, 56, 76, 89, 91
directors, 11
displacement, 13, 14, 16, 17, 18, 19, 20, 23
dissatisfaction, 12
distribution, 14, 52, 56, 63, 72, 80
dominance, 50
Dominican Republic, 12, 53

dynamism, viii, 26, 28

E

East Asia, 52, 60, 70, 73, 76, 80, 82
Eastern Europe, 6, 30
economic growth, 2, 3, 5, 6, 49
economies of scale, 50, 56
education, 7, 10, 11
educational system, 2, 4, 6
El Salvador, 53, 73
electronic data interchange (EDI), 52
employees, vii, viii, 1, 3, 5, 16, 19, 26, 28, 30, 36, 37, 38, 39, 41, 42, 43, 44, 45, 46, 47, 48, 58, 63, 72, 74, 77, 78, 79, 81, 87, 90, 91, 94
employers, 1, 6, 7, 12, 13, 14
employment, vii, 1, 2, 3, 4, 5, 7, 8, 9, 10, 21, 23, 26, 27, 28, 35, 36, 37, 38, 39, 41, 42, 44, 45, 46, 47, 48, 49, 50, 56, 57, 58, 62, 63, 69, 72, 74, 83, 87, 90, 91, 94, 95
employment opportunities, vii, 1, 3
endogeneity, 47
energy, 28
energy input, 28
engineering, 7, 9, 19, 20, 31, 32, 33, 56, 65, 74, 75, 82, 91
environment, 59
equipment, 31, 36, 39, 41, 49, 62, 70, 88, 90
equity, 76, 79
erosion, 51, 95
Europe, 6, 30, 52, 68, 76
evidence, 7, 29, 31, 82
evolution, 52, 65, 70
execution, 73
expenditures, 80, 81
expertise, 55, 65, 95
exports, 52, 60
extraction, 18

F

fabrication, 70, 71, 72, 74, 76, 81, 82, 94
face-to-face interaction, 23
factories, 52, 54, 60
FAS, 91
FDI, 32, 37, 41, 52, 56, 67, 76, 86, 89
FDI inflow, 41
fear, 12, 16
federal employment, 2
financial, 2, 7, 8, 9, 18, 19, 20, 61
firm size, 27, 29, 72
fishing, 15, 17, 18
fixed costs, 80
flexibility, 76, 85
fluctuations, 19
footwear, 38
Ford, 63
foregone employment opportunities, vii, 1, 3
foreign companies, 20, 26, 29, 32, 34, 48, 77
foreign direct investment, 3, 32, 34, 37, 41, 56, 76, 89, 91
foreign firms, 34, 76
foreign investment, 56, 80

G

GDP, 49
Germany, 68
global competition, 70, 72, 82
globalization, 2, 4, 27, 82
goods and services, 3, 4, 21
government intervention, 5
Grenada, 53
Gross Domestic Product, 83
growth, 3, 4, 5, 10, 20, 26, 28, 38, 46, 47, 49, 54, 57, 58, 59, 60, 62, 64, 69, 70, 72, 79, 94
Guatemala, 53
guidance, 2, 13, 48
guidelines, 28
Guyana, 53

H

Haiti, 53
health, viii, 11, 18, 26, 28
health services, 18

higher education, 10
Honduras, 53
Hong Kong, 53, 60, 73, 79
hospitality, 18
housing, 19, 20
Hungary, 6
hypothesis, 33, 34, 41, 46, 47, 77

I

identification, 28
identity, 60
implicit knowledge, 56
import penetration, 36, 88
imports, 34, 36, 51, 52, 55, 64, 75, 88, 89, 91
improvements, 62
incidence, 14, 16, 19
income support, 5, 21
independent variable, 41, 46
India, 2, 6, 12, 21, 53, 76, 78
individuals, 2, 4, 6
Indonesia, 53
inductor, 48
industrial chemicals, 89
industrialized countries, 49, 52
industries, 2, 3, 4, 5, 9, 10, 13, 14, 18, 19, 20, 21, 26, 27, 28, 31, 32, 33, 34, 35, 36, 37, 38, 40, 41, 42, 46, 47, 48, 49, 54, 56, 59, 64, 65, 70, 80, 81, 82, 87, 88, 89, 90, 93, 94, 95
industry, 2, 4, 5, 6, 7, 10, 11, 14, 16, 18, 19, 23, 26, 27, 28, 29, 30, 31, 32, 33, 34, 35, 36, 37, 38, 39, 40, 41, 42, 44, 45, 46, 47, 48, 49, 50, 52, 53, 54, 56, 59, 62, 63, 64, 66, 67, 68, 70, 71, 72, 73, 75, 76, 77, 79, 80, 81, 82, 83, 87, 88, 89, 90, 91, 94, 95
information technology, 2, 6, 32, 51
infrastructure, 52
institutions, 95
integrated circuits, 70, 77, 78, 82
integration, 2, 6, 30, 66, 70
intellectual property, 55
intermediaries, 54
international trade, 4, 30
investment, 4, 29, 33, 35, 52, 56, 73, 80
investments, 21, 73, 74, 76, 78, 89, 94
investors, 7
iron, 38
issues, viii, 5, 26, 28, 29, 31, 37, 46, 47, 48, 77, 83, 90, 93
Italy, 53

J

Jamaica, 53
Japan, 52, 70, 71, 76
job creation, 3
job loss, vii, 1, 2, 3, 4, 13, 14, 16, 17, 18, 19, 20, 21, 57, 73
jobless, 3
Jordan, 6

K

Korea, 53, 60

L

labor market, 3, 13, 16, 17, 23
landscape, 48, 70, 71
Latin America, 73
laws, 4
layoffs, 3, 14, 16, 20
lead, 51, 70
leadership, 12, 76
leakage, 7
level of education, 7
life sciences, 7, 32
light, 10, 14, 29, 81
Lithuania, 6
loans, 7
logistics, 55
lower prices, 4

M

magnitude, 13, 42
majority, 6, 10, 29, 31, 54, 62, 63

management, 12, 21, 30, 51, 52, 55, 61, 71, 76, 78
manufacturing, viii, 2, 3, 5, 6, 9, 11, 13, 14, 19, 26, 28, 29, 30, 31, 32, 33, 35, 36, 38, 41, 48, 49, 50, 52, 54, 55, 56, 57, 58, 59, 60, 61, 62, 64, 65, 67, 70, 71, 76, 78, 79, 80, 81, 82, 83, 88, 89, 93, 94, 95
manufacturing firms, viii, 26, 28, 48, 49, 57
market share, 51, 59, 62, 71, 77
marketing, 55, 76, 77, 78, 80
mass, 14, 20, 30, 51, 53, 55
materials, 48, 68, 69
medical, 9
memory, 70, 78, 94
metropolitan areas, 9
Mexico, 6, 13, 53, 66, 67, 68, 73
Middle East, 12
migration, 49, 81
military, 54
minimum wage, 4
Minneapolis, 9
missions, 2, 5
models, 12, 41, 42, 46, 82, 94
motivation, 80
multinational corporations, 3, 5
music, 11

N

nanotechnology, 7
National Association of Manufacturers, 86
national product, 89
national unemployment rate, vii, 1, 3, 14
negative relation, 47
Netherlands, 53, 76
networking, 78
next generation, 82
Nicaragua, 53
North American Industrial Classification System (NAICS), 35, 93

O

occupational groups, 9
officials, 25
offshore outsourcing, vii, 1, 3, 4, 5, 12, 26, 28, 61, 64
operations, 5, 8, 9, 11, 18, 29, 31, 32, 54, 59, 63, 67, 69, 75, 76, 80, 81
opportunities, vii, 1, 3, 32, 33
original equipment manufacturers' (OEMs), 31
outsourcing, iv, vii, viii, 1, 2, 3, 4, 5, 12, 26, 27, 28, 29, 30, 31, 32, 34, 35, 39, 40, 53, 59, 61, 64, 65, 70, 76, 80, 82, 88, 93
oversight, 12, 30

P

Pakistan, 12
Panama, 53
parallel, 74
participants, 48
patents, viii, 26, 28, 37, 90
payroll, 9, 75
peer review, 28
petroleum, 38, 48
pharmaceutical, 81
Philippines, 6, 13, 53
photographers, 11
plants, 32, 60, 67, 68, 74, 93
plastics, 36, 88
playing, 4
police, 23
policymakers, vii, 1, 3, 4, 29
population, 13
positive correlation, 40
postal service, 11
preparation, 41
President, 84
probability, 16
process control, 71
process innovation, viii, 26, 28, 79
producers, 51, 64, 76, 78, 80, 82
product design, 7, 31, 65, 66, 70, 77
production costs, 71
professionals, 16
project, 30, 37
prosperity, 49, 77
public policy, vii, 1, 3, 4

publishing, 23, 41, 49

Q

query, 7
quotas, 52, 60

R

radio, 23
real estate, 14, 15, 17
recession, vii, 1, 2, 3, 4, 6, 14, 16, 17, 19, 20, 63, 72
recovery, 3, 14, 16, 17, 23
regression, 28, 34, 41, 42, 46
regression analysis, 28, 46
regression model, 41
relevance, 41
requirements, 10, 72
research and development (R&D), 32
researchers, 9, 48
resilience, 57
resources, 18
response, 1, 6, 7, 29, 52, 54, 61, 65, 82
response time, 52, 54, 61
restructuring, 13
retail, 14, 15, 17, 18, 55, 56, 89
revenue, 81
risk, 5, 6, 7, 9, 10, 13, 14, 16, 17, 19, 20, 35
Russia, 6

S

safety, 4, 11, 13
Samsung, 94
savings, 12, 75
scaling, 54
science, 10, 37, 90, 91
scope, 40
secondary data, 48
security, 2, 6, 12, 14, 16, 21
semiconductors, 28, 49, 70, 71, 72, 73, 78, 80, 82
service provider, vii, 1, 3, 12, 14
services, 1, 2, 3, 4, 5, 6, 7, 8, 9, 11, 12, 13, 14, 16, 18, 19, 20, 22, 26, 28, 31, 33, 70, 74, 76, 81, 95
shareholders, 4
SIC, 28, 35, 36, 37, 38, 39, 41, 43, 44, 46, 47, 55, 57, 63, 64, 73, 75, 87, 88, 89, 90, 91, 93, 94
Silicon Valley, 77
Singapore, 12, 74, 94
skilled workers, 73
small businesses, 29, 32, 33, 34, 36, 37, 47, 48, 87
small firms, viii, 26, 27, 28, 29, 35, 38, 41, 42, 46, 47, 48, 50, 56, 63, 77, 82, 87, 94
Small manufacturers, viii, 26, 28, 38, 62, 83
social network, 95
social sciences, 9
software, 2, 7, 9, 11, 12
South Korea, 53, 71
specialists, 10, 11
specifications, 68, 94
state, 4, 76
steel, 38
stock price, 4
storage, 90
structural characteristics, 2, 4, 71
supplier, 31, 62, 65, 67, 68
suppliers, viii, 26, 28, 31, 32, 34, 52, 54, 59, 62, 64, 65, 66, 67, 68, 69, 80, 89, 93
supply chain, 31, 32, 51, 52, 62, 66, 76
support services, 2

T

Taiwan, 53, 60, 74, 78
talent, 12, 74, 75
technical writers, 9
techniques, 41, 49, 71, 83
technological advances, 2, 52
technologies, 6, 52, 67, 70
technology, 2, 6, 32, 37, 51, 70, 79, 90
telecommunications, 16, 23, 70
testing, 70, 71, 72, 76, 78
textbook, 49
textiles, 49, 50

time periods, 28, 34, 37, 38
time series, 35
Title I, 21
tobacco, 49
Toyota, 32, 67
trade, 4, 14, 15, 17, 18, 20, 26, 28, 30, 36, 52, 66, 81, 87
trade deficit, 20
traditions, 68
transformation, 49
transmission, 2, 6
transplant, 67, 69
transportation, 18
Trinidad and Tobago, 53

U

U.S. borders, 3
U.S. Bureau of Labor Statistics, 2, 3, 14, 18, 20, 23
U.S. Department of Commerce, 53, 83, 86
U.S. Department of Labor, 51, 84, 85
U.S. economy, 4, 13, 74
U.S. manufacturers, iv, vii, 1, 3, 22, 32, 70
Ukraine, 6
unemployment rate, vii, 1, 3, 14
United, vii, 1, 2, 3, 4, 5, 6, 7, 8, 12, 13, 16, 20, 21, 26, 27, 29, 31, 32, 33, 48, 52, 54, 55, 66, 67, 70, 71, 73, 74, 76, 77, 78, 80, 81, 82, 83, 84, 86, 89, 91, 93, 94
United Kingdom, 6
United Nations, 21, 86
United States, vii, 1, 2, 3, 4, 5, 6, 7, 8, 12, 13, 16, 20, 21, 26, 27, 29, 31, 32, 33, 48, 52, 54, 55, 66, 67, 70, 71, 73, 76, 77, 78, 80, 81, 82, 83, 84, 89, 91, 93

V

variables, 35, 41, 42, 46, 87, 94
variations, 38, 40, 41, 94
vehicles, 49, 62, 93
Vietnam, 53
vulnerability, 2, 10

W

wage differentials, 12
Washington, 9, 20, 22, 23, 83, 84, 85, 86
Western Europe, 76
white-collar workers, 2, 6, 7, 13, 14, 16, 21, 23
wholesale, 14, 81
WIA, 21
Wisconsin, 85
wood, 49
workers, vii, 1, 2, 3, 4, 5, 6, 7, 9, 10, 11, 13, 14, 15, 16, 17, 18, 19, 20, 21, 23, 72, 74, 77, 81
Workforce Investment Act, 21

Y

yield, 27